MOBILE LEARNING MINDSET

THE DISTRICT LEADER'S GUIDE TO IMPLEMENTATION

CARL HOOKER

International Society for Technology in Education
EUGENE, OREGON • ARLINGTON, VIRGINIA

Mobile Learning Mindset
The District Leader's Guide to Implementation
Carl Hooker

Editor: *Paul Wurster*
Associate Editor: *Emily Reed*
Production Manager: *Christine Longmuir*
Copy Editor: *Kristin Landon*
Proofreader: *Ann Skaugset*
Cover Design: *Brianne Beigh*
Book Design and Production: *Kim McGovern*

Library of Congress Cataloging-in-Publication Data

Names: Hooker, Carl, author.
  Title: Mobile learning mindset : The district leader's guide to implementation / Carl Hooker.
  Description: Eugene : International Society for Technology in Education, [2015]
  Identifiers: LCCN 2015047881| ISBN 9781564843739 (pbk.) | ISBN 9781564845788 (epub) | ISBN 9781564845795 (pdf)
  Subjects: LCSH: Mobile communication systems in education. | School districts—Administration.
  Classification: LCC LB1044.84 .H66 2016 | DDC 371.33—dc23 LC record available at http://lccn.loc.gov/2015047881

First Edition
ISBN: 978-1-56484-373-9
Ebook version available.

Printed in the United States of America

ISTE® is a registered trademark of the International Society for Technology in Education.

About ISTE

The International Society for Technology in Education (ISTE) is the premier nonprofit organization serving educators and education leaders committed to empowering connected learners in a connected world. ISTE serves more than 100,000 education stakeholders throughout the world.

ISTE's innovative offerings include the ISTE Conference & Expo, one of the biggest, most comprehensive ed tech events in the world—as well as the widely adopted ISTE Standards for learning, teaching and leading in the digital age and a robust suite of professional learning resources, including webinars, online courses, consulting services for schools and districts, books, and peer-reviewed journals and publications. Visit iste.org to learn more.

About the Author

Photo Courtesy
Manny Pandya

Carl Hooker has been involved in education since graduating from the University of Texas in 1998. He has been in a variety of positions in both Austin Independent School District (ISD) and Eanes ISD, from first grade teacher to virtualization coordinator.

Hooker is director of innovation and digital learning in Eanes ISD. He is also the founder of the learning festival iPadpalooza (http://ipadpalooza. com). As director, he makes use of his background in both education and technology to bring a unique vision to the district and its programs. During his time in the position, the district has jumped into social media, adopted Google Apps for Education, and started to build a paperless environment with Google Docs. He helped spearhead the Learning and Engaging through Access and Personalization (LEAP) program, which put 1:1 iPads into the hands of all K–12 students at Eanes.

Since becoming an educator, Hooker has been a part of a strong educational shift with technology integration. From his start as a teacher to his current district technology leadership, he has always held one common belief—kids need to drive their own learning. He realizes the challenges in our current public educational institutions and meets them head on. His unique blend of educational background, technical expertise, and humor make him a successful driving force for this change. Hooker also works as a keynote speaker and consultant through his company HookerTech, LLC.

Contents

Contents

Preface

In January of 2010, Steve Jobs took the stage at a major Apple event to announce the creation of a device that was in between a laptop and a smartphone. When he announced the iPad, the reviews were mixed. Wasn't this something that had been tried before, even with Apple's MessengerPad (http://en.wikipedia.org/wiki/MessagePad)? How was this going to work in mainstream society when it's bigger and bulkier than a phone and doesn't have the keyboard of a laptop?

At the time of the announcement, I was a virtualization coordinator for the district. The technology director (my boss at the time) looked at me with wonder when I got excited over this announcement. This is going to change the face of education, I told him. His response was, "I bet they don't sell even a million of them. It's like a crappy version of a laptop, only you can only do one thing at a time on it. It doesn't even have a USB port!"

In retrospect, I should have taken that bet, as Apple would go on to sell a million in pre-order sales alone. Flash forward a few more months. On April 2, I would get a promotion to the role of director of instructional technology. The next day the first-generation iPad would be sold in U.S. stores. I point this all out to say that even with all the prep work and sweat necessary for a successful device deployment, some synergy is also required.

As director of instructional technology, I was taking over a dying role of sorts. Many districts were cutting the position at that time in Texas, and some felt it was a "nice to have" more than "a need to have" position. Knowing that going in, I made it one of my personal missions to erase the thought in the minds of the purse-string holders that my position could ever be seen as obsolete. In fact, I set out to do the exact opposite: make them think they can't function successfully without it.

A big part of any leadership position is assessing risks. With the announcement of the iPad, my mind immediately went to education. How could these devices help students personalize their own learning? How would they enhance engagement and the learning experience of kids? Are those gains in engagement and personalization enough to warrant giving every student one of these devices?

These questions plus many others went through my mind and those of many of the leaders in my district in the months to come. Ultimately, we tried a small pilot of six iPads at the Westlake High School library to see what students and teachers thought. They were extremely well received, but with a bond just failing in the fall of 2010, the hope of ever getting more of them in the hands of students seemed hopeless.

Enter the second synergistic event. A group of leaders including myself made a trip to Cupertino, California, for an executive briefing on what Apple's thoughts were on iPads in education. Before lunch on the first day, the Westlake High School principal leaned over and said to us, "We need one of these for every student." At that time, iPads were considered purely consumptive devices, a nice way to read a book or take notes but nothing in the way of creation. That trip to Apple's headquarters changed all of that for those in the room that were skeptical.

When we returned, we went on to expand the pilot to around 70 different users. From special education students to principals to high school AP teachers, we had as many key stakeholders as possible get their hands on these devices to put them through the paces. At this point the iPad 2 had just launched and had a lot more functionality on the creation end than its predecessor, namely the addition of a camera.

The pilot would go on to expand into Westlake High School the following fall and eventually expand to all 8,000 Eanes ISD students (K–12) by the spring of 2013. Here's an early blog post right after the launch of the pilot on the EanesWifi site: http://bit.ly/1K1x0lq.html. Along the way, I've seen the highs and lows of having a device for every student, especially one as nimble and easy to use as an iPad.

This book isn't so much about the device as it is all the things we learned along the way. There are examples and activities throughout the chapters to help a leader heading into a mobile device implementation or some ideas for adjustment if you've already started one. Some of these are interactive and will actually encourage you to take out your own device (if you are reading it in paper form) and interact. While some of the examples will be iPad-specific, I took care in making sure the tools and strategies for visionary leaders can be used no matter what the device.

What I hope you gain from this book is a better understanding of what effect mobile devices have on your staff, your students, and your community. With a better understanding of mobile learning, the tools and activities throughout the book will help you with modeling, risk-taking, building a culture of creativity and shared ownership, and how to interact and lead the various components of a mobile device initiative.

As mentioned in the introduction, five other books in the series are written with a focus on different key areas when it comes to mobile learning. While each of the six books stands on its own, I feel that having the set will give all parties involved a better understanding of each other and can help create some common language and goals to help our students with their learning. After all, we are now at least 15% of the way through the 21st century. It's about time we stopped talking about 21st-century learning and actually started doing something about it.

Good luck, and thank you for being a part of this mobile learning revolution!

—*Carl Hooker*

INTRODUCTION

District leaders are faced with many decisions throughout their time as administrators. Some decisions are a reaction to a problem. Other decisions are proactive to avoid a problem or open up an opportunity. Whatever the reason behind these decisions, a leader must have a clear idea of the district vision. But even more important than understanding that vision is communicating it to all the key stakeholders in their organization.

In a mobile learning initiative, this means working with campus administrators on setting proper expectations for both teachers and students. This means spending the time and money to support the vision by valuing professional learning. It means showcasing the effective use of mobile devices by teachers and students. It means communicating with parents and the community on the value of having mobile devices in the classroom for learning. And it means providing resources (including funds) for the technical support that comes with introducing several hundred or several thousand devices into a school environment.

How to Use This Book

This book will be broken down into various chapters that will serve as both a guide and a resource at times during various stages of your mobile learning initiative. The structure of the chapters in this book will mirror the structure of the other books in the series, though the content will differ.

The first chapter about vision is all about the "why." Part of having a successful mobile learning initiative is identifying why you are setting off down this path for your district, and then effectively communicating that "why" to all constituents. There will be plenty of time to spend on both the "how" and "what" of a mobile learning initiative, but not having a firm grasp on why you are doing all of this could spell doom down the road.

The second chapter is dedicated to that exact "doom" I just spoke about. It outlines the top 10 things *not* to do in a mobile learning initiative from the viewpoint of a district leader. Every school district is different and has a different set of values, which makes giving advice a tricky subject to maneuver. However, identifying (and avoiding) common pitfalls can go a long way toward making the initiative a success.

Chapter 3 is an interview with Patrick Larkin, assistant superintendent for learning in Burlington Public Schools in Massachusetts. He's been running a successful mobile device initiative for years in the Northeast and has been recognized globally as a visionary in the new mobile learning world. While much of the book is based on my perspectives and dealings with various district mobile learning initiatives, this chapter is meant to bring in a different perspective and answer lingering questions that I encounter while working with other leaders. I was particularly excited to hear why Patrick decided to move his desk out of his office and into the hallway! These interviews are also captured on video via Google Hangout and are available to view if you'd like to watch the unabridged version.

The middle chapters really delve deeply into strategies and examples of what leaders in mobile learning initiatives do well to succeed. Keeping the end in mind is important, as well as weathering the storm of the inevitable "implementation dip." Building a brand that you can market and garner support for is important when attempting to unite a district and community. The idea of creating a culture that encourages risk taking is often bandied about these days, but what does that really look like, and how do leaders take risks and still be successful? Chapter 6 deals with that quandary that all leaders face, as the egos and fear of failure tend to increase the higher up the proverbial ladder administrators travel.

As we work our way into the later chapters, we'll look at ways to cultivate a true feeling of shared ownership around a mobile learning initiative and why that's important. We'll also look at how a visionary leader must not only be willing to take risks but also model this new learning direction in their everyday life. Chapter 8 focuses on the importance of modeling as a leader, and it provides some examples of ways to do that in a way that packs a punch.

In the penultimate chapter, we'll explore how the role of the district leader interacts with the other main players in a mobile learning initiative. It's one thing to have strong campus leaders, but how do you hire those? Also, how do you make professional learning a focus and help the teachers with the day-to-day interactions in the classroom? Parents and community can make a mobile learning initiative sink or swim based on their support or opposition. A district leader needs to dedicate a large chunk of time to visiting, listening, supporting, and even training the parents to make the initiative a success.

In the final chapter, we'll focus on the importance of reflection and sharing of ideas. Many have traveled the road to 1:1 or BYOD, but if everyone shares their experiences, we all benefit from the collective wisdom. However, if we don't share what we have learned and mistakes we have made, we could potentially be hurting other students even if they aren't in our district. No leader wants that on their conscience, so in Chapter 10 we'll cover how to share and what to share and still be considered a genuine, truthful administrator.

"Easter Eggs"

According to Wikipedia, an Easter egg is "an inside joke, hidden message, or feature in an interactive work such as a computer program, video game or DVD menu screen." Why can't we also have these in books? In this book, I've hidden several Easter eggs that you'll have to uncover and discover. Some are buried in words, others in images. How do you reveal them? If you are reading this book in paper form, you'll need to download the Aurasma app (www.aurasma.com) and find the trigger images to unlock the Easter eggs. Find and follow the "MLM Vision" channel to make it all work. Happy hunting!

CHAPTER 1

STARTING WITH THE "WHY"

One of the most influential videos during my time as an administrator early in our initiative was Simon Sinek's TED talk titled "How great leaders inspire action" (http://tinyurl.com/o8jswn4). In the talk, Sinek discusses what he calls the "Golden Circle" of what makes certain people or companies successful (see Figure 1.1). The root of his talk (and later his first book) is that as leaders we must always focus our attention on the "Why" whenever starting a project or initiative.

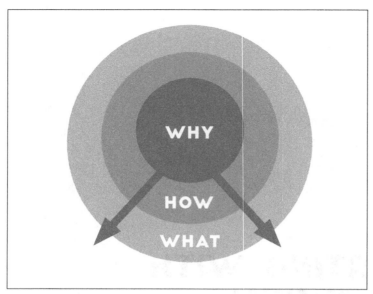

Figure 1.1 Simon Sinek's Golden Circle.

I found this talk extremely compelling, especially when I first watched it. At the time, we were in the throes of a debate about what device we should choose for our 1:1 mobile device initiative. Lots of time and energy were dedicated to this "What" of the initiative, while equal amounts of time and energy neglected the "Why." Ultimately, we discovered the error in our ways and refocused our energy on why we were doing this in the first place.

As a leader, you will need to communicate this message clearly and well to all stakeholders. Everyone from a teacher to a parent to a student should know what the purpose of learning with mobile devices is in your district. Creating a vision or goal out of the "Why" will help guide all other parts of the initiative. In this book, we'll look at why having a strong and well-communicated vision is so important and discuss the role a leader plays in a district that is embracing mobile learning.

Many districts have a mission or vision statement. If I had to hazard a guess, it's a buzz-filled sentence or paragraph about pushing kids toward excellence and making learning personalized for each student. Most, if not all, usually contain some statement about becoming global learners or using the 4 C's of 21st-century learning in the classrooms. The bottom line is, districts put this type of language in their mission statements but rarely have an action plan to follow through with it.

Any district starting out with a mobile learning initiative needs to look long and hard at these statements. Do they need to be adjusted? Can the goals of the initiative align with the goals of the district? Our district's mission statement mentions having students globally learn in a "technology-rich environment." So, although there may be differences in opinion about what that means, I always point to that statement when discussing why we are doing a mobile device initiative.

It's also important to have some measurable goals in mind when you are setting out on this mission. You might take the bait and decide to tie your mobile device initiative to test scores. I've seen districts go this route to improve writing or math or science scores. The thinking is the introduction of mobile devices will "auto-magically" make the scores rise as the students will have more access to technology (neglecting any thought that pedagogy might actually play a part in that, too). Although I think test scores do play a role in measuring school districts, scores don't necessarily measure the impact of learning. Judy Estrin writes in her book *Closing the Innovation Gap: Reigniting the Spark of Creativity in the Global Economy* (McGraw-Hill, 2008) that innovative companies like Pixar steer clear of measurements for the most part. While you can have metrics that will measure small, incremental components of your initiative (such as student engagement or communication), it's not feasible to associate test scores with that innovation. In fact, Estrin goes on to write that innovation geared toward the future can't be measured while it's actually happening.

That's a good lesson for an administrator leading a 1:1 initiative. The long-term goals and measurements can't be fully obtained until students have left the institution. Before our initiative, one of the first bits of feedback we got from students who had graduated was that although we prepared them for the academia of college, they weren't prepared for all the digital distractions that would be surrounding them. Alumni would share that they would sit in

300-seat lecture halls and witness all the students with multiple devices half-paying attention to the professor and half-paying attention to their device.

In the college setting, most professors believe that it's the job of the student to learn—more so than it is the professor's job to make sure they learn. So students leaving a fairly device-restrictive, nurturing environment are suddenly thrust into a world with no support and no boundaries. While this could be the case for most students heading to college, we saw an opportunity to help with at least one part of this issue. Teaching students at an early age to manage digital distraction, while a disruption in the early stages, was a major goal of our initiative in the hopes that students would be more than college-ready—they would be college-successful.

One of the most powerful graphics I've ever come across was from Tracy Clark (@tracyclark08) and her "S'more" she created called "measuring what matters." When CEOs at Fortune 500 companies were asked what they want most in future employees, the words that they repeated the most were represented in her "Soft Skills Bingo" card (see Figure 1.2). What stands out to me right away isn't so much what you see, but what you don't see. I don't see "good at math" or "proficient in writing" or even "good with Microsoft Office." You see skills like perseverance, resilience, teamwork, leadership, and those 4 C's we hear about so often (collaboration, communication, critical thinking, and creativity). These "future-ready" skills, as I refer to them, are much more important to the future of our kids, so shouldn't we focus on these?

As we are now proceeding into the fourth year of our initiative, these skills are the ones we are focused on measuring going forward. While there is no true "21st-century skills" assessment, there are a few out there on the market that could accomplish the task. When done in conjunction with portfolios, observation, and qualitative surveys, you could really start to measure how these skills are being taught in a classroom. Although technology isn't a specific skill listed here, it certainly affects most areas of this bingo card.

So before you move forward through this book, be thinking about what skills are the most future-necessary for your students and how your initiative can help build those skills. If at all possible, have a pre-assessment based on these skills so you can have some comparative data (one of my top 10 things *not* to do, as we failed to do this from the outset). Keeping this at the forefront of your mission not only will drive the change, it will give leadership, teachers, students, and parents a clear vision of what is expected and what the goals of your mobile device initiative are.

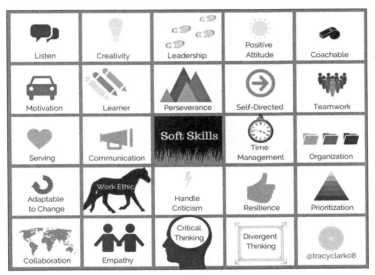

Figure 1.2 Tracy Clark's S'more "Measuring What Matters" (https://www.smore.com/bg57). Courtesy Tracy Clark.

CHAPTER 2

TOP 10 THINGS NOT TO DO

Sometimes the best advice is to tell people what to avoid. Every district and school is different. There is different parent support, demographic makeup, teacher readiness, technology proficiency, and campus leadership expectations. This top 10 list should be a warning list for district leaders who are either starting or currently implementing a mobile device initiative. Please know that this chapter could easily be 20 things, but these 10 items are the most crucial to avoid when embarking on this journey as a leader.

1. Do *Not* Forget to Model

You are setting the vision and preaching what it will do; it's time to put your money where your mouth is and model this change. This means using the exact same device the students and teachers are using during meetings, site visits, and community meetings. That type of modeling shows that you not only believe in what you are doing, but you are also a part of this change (see Figure 2.1).

Some early examples of modeling include insisting that all leadership staff and school board members have the same device and that they use these devices during all meetings. Also, if you expect teachers to attend trainings that focus on the device and how to integrate it into the curriculum, you should be present for these same trainings. Many superintendents or school leaders assign professional development to staff, but don't attend themselves. Learning alongside your staff sends a powerful message that you value the investment of their time to learn about it.

Figure 2.1 The author trying to be a model mobile DJ.

2. Do *Not* Neglect Buy-In

That might be a bit of a double-negative there, but you get my point. How many district initiatives or incredible ideas are hatched and thrown onto campuses without any buy-in by the staff? This is a recipe for failure. Seek out the leaders and respected voices on campus to be a part of this process *before* you even start the initiative. This means bringing community members and teacher leaders together early on to discuss the "why."

Listen to their ideas, concerns, and solutions respectfully and openly. While not all the ideas may be yours, it's amazing how much better an initiative like this will run when people feel like they have ownership in part of the process. One thing our superintendent does during a major decision is to leave the room when final discussions need to take place.

He's there to handle the questions and arguments, but when it comes time to build consensus around a particular decision, he walks out and tells the committee or group that he'll be back in 30 minutes and listen to their solution. This yields two very positive outcomes:

1. Teachers and staff in the committee feel empowered to make a decision and stand behind it because it was not handed down from "on high." If someone questions the decision, they will defend it and even take it somewhat personally.

2. Should questions arise about why the district decided on a particular platform or device, you have evidence that not only was it not just from you, you actually weren't even in the room when the decision was made. Your job is to support the decision of the consensus.

3. Do *Not* Forget to Communicate with Everyone All the Time

While it's certainly possible to over communicate, we are much more guilty in education and administration of under communicating. Collection day for the iPads? Oh yeah, we sent out an email a couple weeks ago about that. Restrictions on the student iPads? We put that info on our single website for everything iPad. No matter what you are doing, 1:1 or otherwise, be prepared to communicate in multiple media with multiple distributions and repetitions. Spreading the word will help decrease confusion and frustration and increase trust and clarity. Too often the mythical "district" is to blame for bad ideas or solutions not communicated.

4. Do *Not* Expect Teaching and Learning to Change Immediately

Much like the image I have pictured in Figure 2.2, just adding technology to a situation won't change anything without support, time, and expectations. Look at the movement around interactive whiteboards in the mid-2000s. These were seen as innovative teaching tools, but the majority of teachers who used them simply made more interactive PowerPoint presentations. That's not really transforming learning, is it?

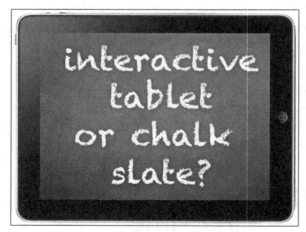

Figure 2.2 Is this transformative teaching?

I have long been preaching Ruben Puentedura's substitution, augmentation, modification, and redefinition (SAMR) model. SAMR (www.hippasus.com/rrpweblog) is a framework through which you can assess and evaluate the technology you use in your class. The SAMR model supports and enables teachers to design, develop, and infuse digital learning experiences that use technology. The goal is to transform learning experiences so they result in higher levels of achievement for students. Apple has also relied heavily on this model, and they see the power in using transformative learning along with powerful tools as a win for students.

Teachers can't be expected to change the way they teach overnight. However, most of the tools we've given them in the past (Smartboards, document cameras, etc.) were teaching tools. This tool is in the hands of kids, which means it's student driven. Teachers and students will lean heavily on substitution in the SAMR model to start, but have patience. Redefinition of teaching and learning does not happen overnight.

One other thing I'll mention is the generation gap of learners in our own schools. Students who have played the "game of school" long enough will see a mobile device initiative as disruptive change, too. This is especially true for high school students who have mastered the art of scoring well on tests, getting homework done, and reading their textbook nightly. Introducing a concept like student-centered learning with a mobile device means not only do they have to do more work, but they also can't just coast by on the older systems of traditional school. I've argued that there is a generation gap in schools between the 5-year-olds just now entering who have been immersed in this world, and the 17-year-olds leaving who have mastered the traditional methods of "learning" in schools. In the new mobile-device-saturated environment where students are empowered to be creative and solve critical problems, they may actually learn more as a result. But it's still a change to consider from the students' perspective nonetheless, and one that doesn't happen overnight.

5. Do *Not* Assume the Entire Community Will Be on Board

As great as the idea behind personalized learning can be, it can be a severe mind-shift for people in the community. Add to that budget cuts with staff time, and you can see how this can quickly turn into a no-win scenario.

It's important to stress what the goals are in all of this, and also to get both parents and teachers working with you to find solutions to little problems (See Figure 2.3). However, that doesn't mean you give them the option to not participate.

Figure 2.3 Parent workshops will help educate your community.

The most successful 1:1 programs have created a universal understanding and expectation across the district about why 1:1 is being done and what it can and should accomplish. While much has been made of the failure of Los Angeles Unified School District's $1.3 billion iPad initiative (http://tinyurl. com/nx2b6qa), it is a cautionary tale about how taking risks can be bad if the concept, or "why" as mentioned in Chapter 1, isn't really addressed or communicated to the community as a whole.

Being open to the community and allowing multiple avenues and forums for them to voice their concerns may not be the most comfortable situation, but these avenues will keep you and the district informed of issues before they get out of control. They also send a message of transparency and shared ownership around a program like this.

6. Do *Not* Overlook the Role of the Campus Leader

Dr. Anthony Muhammad, a building leader turned educational consultant, has said that the single most important member of a district to get something off the ground is the campus administrator. They hold the keys to setting campus expectations and communicating the goals and objectives to their staff. They also are the front line for parent and teacher concerns.

In leading a mobile device initiative, a campus administrator can either champion or sabotage the effort with just a few words. In our district, we had two middle schools with the same demographics and size. One was much more successful with the 1:1 initiative than the other. How could this be? They had similar teachers, similar students, and similar infrastructure. The biggest difference was campus leadership.

On Campus A, the leader introduced the concept of our iPad initiative by telling the staff, "The district has decided to embark on a 1:1 initiative." The administrator of Campus B introduced it this way: "I'm excited that we are expanding our mobile device initiative to our campus! This is a great opportunity for our students, and I expect great things will come from it."

While both leaders had the same announcement to make to their staff, the way those messages were handled made it glaringly obvious to the staff who was on board with this and who wasn't. A teacher on Campus A might think, "If the campus leader isn't on board with it, why should I be motivated to learn and grow and accept this new method of teaching? After all, change takes a lot of work, and it sounds as if the campus administrator who is directly responsible for my evaluation doesn't even care about it. I think I'll just keep doing what I've been doing, as this too shall pass."

Meanwhile, a teacher on Campus B might think, "Wow, this sounds like an interesting change that could be exciting and benefit our students. I know it'll take a lot of work, but it sounds like my administrator is on board and very supportive of it, so I should be, too."

Needless to say, Campus A struggled mightily with this change, and some teachers didn't even take the devices out of their desk drawer for the first semester. Eventually, the leader on Campus A was replaced with a new leader who had high expectations for the staff. The new leader was a big supporter of the initiative because he saw the benefits to student learning, and a teacher who wasn't willing to change for that cause was either shown ways to improve or shown the door.

7. Do *Not* Make the Device the Focus of the Initiative

Do not focus all of your energy and attention around the device. We'll get into this more in the chapter about branding, but it's also important to not center your logo or initiative's acronym around a device. Some poor examples include "iLearn" or "Chromebooks for the Classroom." Devices come and go, and while there will be plenty of attention paid to whatever device your district chooses (notice I didn't say "you choose"), your focus should be on the learning environment in the classroom.

Creating a focus around the idea of empowering student learning means that whatever device you choose, it's adaptable around this concept. Sustainability is a big concern when you are spending money on devices, and if the change hasn't started to happen by the time your next refresh comes, it will likely die on the vine. Continue to highlight the new role of the student learner in these environments and the improvements to learning that this has brought about.

8. Do *Not* Evaluate the Program Solely with Test Scores

Test scores may be the easiest and most publicized metric to measure student achievement, but they are far from the most accurate when you're talking about changing the culture of learning and customizing a student's school experience through a 1:1 program. Engagement, motivation, collaboration, communication, and the desire to dig deeper into subjects were all items we measured through anonymous student and teacher surveys. With all of those improvements, it's what happens next when the student goes on to college and post-college life that's a thousand times more important than how they did on a random test. This item is closely tied to item six—your expectations as the campus leader. Remember this when talking to the community about how the program is going.

As I'll dive into more deeply in the chapters on end goals and reflection, you do need to have some metrics to measure how you are doing along this journey. This doesn't (and shouldn't) be centered around test scores, but your end goals and outcomes need to be fully shared at the onset and continually reviewed, evaluated, and adjusted throughout.

9. Do *Not* Launch a Bunch of Initiatives at Once

People can only change 10% to 15% of themselves in a given year. Teachers are people. Ergo, they can only change or alter 10% to 15% of their teaching practice in any given year. One of the biggest mistakes I see districts make (mine included at one point) is that we propose multiple new concepts at the beginning of the school year. These concepts sound exciting and inspiring at the time, but to staff, they can sound like "one more thing" to learn or do.

Having a culture adaptable to change and new concepts is important, but overloading that culture with constant change will succeed in derailing any initiative you attempt. If your district or campus is embarking on a mobile device initiative, it's a good idea to limit the number of other initiatives taking place. For instance, that probably wouldn't be the best time to institute a new grading policy or a schoolwide writing focus or a districtwide focus on professional learning communities (PLCs). I do see the power in adding these initiatives and possibly integrating them in some way with the mobile device initiative, but having them as add-ons or "one more thing" means they won't be successful, and they'll likely dismantle your mobile device initiative on the way down.

Doing some simple math on those first percentages reveals that it would take 6 to 10 years for a teacher to completely change their pedagogical practice. Introducing a new concept, program, or initiative every year will extend that change out even further.

10. Do *Not* Let Fear Overcome Your Mission

One quote I use often in presentations is from H. P. Lovecraft, who said "The oldest and strongest emotion of mankind is fear, and the oldest and strongest kind of fear is fear of the unknown."

Everyone will go through a phase where they doubt that the idea of a mobile device initiative is working. They'll worry that people will think it's a fad. They'll think it's a waste of money. They'll complain about having to change. They'll worry that the kids will be plugged in all day and just play games. All of these and hundreds of other concerns will be raised throughout the implementation process.

I remember vividly one of our campus administrators calling me the summer before our iPad deployment to tell me that she had just had a nightmare. She was going through the school hallways completely naked and all the students weren't laughing—instead they were taking out their devices and taking pictures. The anxiety level of this administrator was palpable, and there was definitely some fear and doubt entering her mind.

It's easy to get dismayed by the loud minority of critics out there, especially if you already have fear or lack of confidence in what you are doing and why you are doing it. For there to be any hope of your program being successful, the core team of administrators, teachers, and students needs to be on the same page, speaking the same message. That message is plain and simple: This is not a technology expense; it's an investment in our students and their future.

CHAPTER 3

INTERVIEW WITH VISIONARY LEADER PATRICK LARKIN

What follows are excerpts from my interview with Patrick Larkin, assistant superintendent for learning at Burlington Public Schools in Massachusetts. Patrick is an amazing leader who really embodies much of what this book is about. His district has had a mobile learning initiative with iPads for many years, and I first got to work with him in a session at Tech Forum Boston called "Top 20 Things NOT to do in a 1:1" (sound familiar?) Here is a link to the slides from that presentation, if you would like to take a closer look: http://tinyurl.com/p2a8jds.

Patrick Larkin

Although I present the majority of the interview here, I have also provided a link to the Google Hangout recording of our chat at the end of this chapter.

Carl Hooker (CH): What is your official title?

Patrick Larkin (PL): My official title is assistant superintendent for learning in Burlington Public Schools in Massachusetts.

CH: That's a nice title. Now I'm going to ask you what should your title really be? I mean, does that reflect what you do? If you could make up any title you wanted, what would it be?

PL: You know, I kind of like [my title]. I know there are people that have done titles like chief innovation officer. I like the fact that school districts are thinking outside the box, and you know, taking risks for what they call things that make people ask follow-up questions. But I like "assistant superintendent for learning" because that's what we're here for in schools. The thing that I like about it being sort of general is that we're talking about adult learning as well as student learning. I don't think there's a more important thing we do in the district than support our learners, both adult and student. I like it—I'm satisfied with that title.

CH: I like that you included both the adult and student part in your description. Too often they are seen as separate. What's a typical day in your job look like?

PL: One of the nice things about Burlington is that leaders have the flexibility to not have a "typical" day. I get to go out and interact with teachers and students fairly regularly. Of course we still have things in the office doing the "administrivia" stuff we have to do. It's all about being out in the schools. We have six schools, and so it's important to get out there and be visible and be a resource for learners.

CH: I guess I should back up and ask, what kind of initiatives have you done at Burlington when it comes to mobile devices and mobile learning?

PL: We're doing a lot of different things. The elementary schools are 1:1 with grades 1 to 5. In elementary they are in carts and the students use them in centers, for making videos, publications, a lot of project-based learning. At the middle school we are having discussions about students taking the iPads home next year, but it's similar in a lot of ways. We're doing a lot of project-based stuff and creative stuff. Kids just aren't consuming, they are creating things with it. At the high school, it's kind of funny but the older you get with students, the more they are accustomed to traditional schooling. That's not to say there aren't pockets of creativity but generally we see a lot more lower-level SAMR things happening in high school where students are using it for things like notetaking and not quite so innovative. That said, they are pushing the envelope; it just really depends on the particular classroom. Teachers are able to do a lot more blended [learning] with kids because they now have devices in their hands, so teachers are taking advantage of the access at their fingertips.

CH: We saw a lot of that at our high school, too. I wonder if it's a case where risk-taking is encouraged more at earlier ages, but that idea of risk-taking is taken out as students get older. So let me ask you this, we talk a lot about taking risks in education, but what are your thoughts on that concept as a leader?

PL: I definitely think we need to push kids to think outside the box. That's where I really like the title of assistant superintendent for learning because I think a lot of our teachers need permission and to hear it's OK to go out there on a limb and try something new. You can learn a lot more from failing and failing publicly and sharing that [experience] than just going through the traditional routine of school—of "getting through a chapter." We don't care about the stuff in that chapter—we are pushing quality over quantity here. It's funny, we just hosted our first TEDx event through one of our classes. It was a student's "20% time" project. They decided that they wanted to bring a TEDx to Burlington and we just had it this past weekend. We're seeing more and more of those pockets getting larger. Hopefully we'll see [risk-taking] become more of the norm as we move forward.

CH: It's a tricky thing for leadership, taking risks. Do you have an example of maybe when you took a risk and failed?

PL: I'm sure there are so many of them—that's the problem. You fail every day with certain things. I think honestly, if I'm thinking of myself, I have failed to personally integrate the iPad as my tool of choice. I keep working at it and trying it, but it makes me feel like a bit of a hypocrite. I'm the guy pushing to get this in the hands of every student, but I personally defer to my MacBook Air. If I'm pushing this as the primary tool for all the student learners, then myself as one of the lead adult learners should be using that same resource more often. I use it a lot, but honestly I feel like I should be using it a lot more. Honestly, many adults fail because we don't take the time to change our work-flow. Some people think "this is my workflow, I go to the copy machine" but why can't they go paperless? For me, I'm so comfortable using the laptop that even though I know I can do most things on the iPad, I just haven't put in the time to learn it. I'd say that's a pretty big failure for me thus far.

CH: I think you just made the case for 2:1 right there.

PL: There you go! That's more real world right?

CH: Yup.

PL: We are not a 1:1 world anymore so maybe I'm ahead of the curve? (laughs)

CH: There you go! So let me ask you this: You work with a lot of leadership on the campus level. How do you get leaders to be on the same page with you and your vision?

PL: I think one of the biggest things is modeling. I think you'll only go so far on an initiative if you say things like "I want you to do this but I won't do it myself." I know it's not quite as easy for a campus or district administrator to use the tools in the same way, but there are access points and we talk a lot about that. Communication is a good starting point, the way we communicate with our stakeholders outside of our offices. How do we do that? How do we promote best practices for teachers? That communication saves us a lot of headaches because if the community feels like we are accessible and what's going on is transparent, they are more comfortable and happier. I think we have a lot of tools that we as school leaders can use to model best practices and support them in that way.

CH: This is a totally random question, but what's the coolest thing in your office?

PL: I don't have an office, to be honest with you.

CH: Really? Tell me about that.

PL: When I was a high school principal about 5 years ago, I decided that I wasn't going to have an office anymore, so I took a desk and put it in the main lobby of the high school. So when I came into central office, there used to be an assistant superintendent, but a couple of years had passed in the interim. When I came in there was a big long space with three curriculum coaches in there. I didn't feel right kicking those people out of their space that they had been in for the last couple of years. So I went and got a stand-up desk and I put it right in the outer "greeting" area of the central office with the secretaries. I'd rather be out there than be locked behind closed doors. I think that's important.

CH: I think that's a big part of getting your vision out there, too—that's great. I have a stand-up desk now too, and it's much healthier than sitting.

PL: Exactly.

CH: What would you say is the most important thing that makes a mobile learning initiative a success? If you had to pick just one thing, what do you think that is?

PL: Student voice or student input. I think students have to be a formal part of the plan and part of the core group of decision makers. Our own experience handicaps us. I've learned so many things that have me almost slapping myself in the face *[slaps self in face]* and saying, "Why didn't I think of that? It's so obvious." I think it's because my own educational background doesn't put those ideas in the forefront of my mind—some of these ideas that the kids come up with. Having students as a part of the decision-making body is imperative.

CH: I think that's a good point that's often overlooked, and I've been guilty of that as well. That's great advice. Let me ask you this: You were talking about failing and sharing the experience. How do you share your experiences, and why do you think it's important to do that?

PL: I share primarily though my blog. I think blogging is the main way to share and then tweet it out and share through all the various social media channels: Google Plus, Twitter, Facebook. That's how I've learned so much from others that were ahead of us in going 1:1 in sharing what they were doing. I just think I owe them a debt of gratitude so that anyone that's coming down the road after us shouldn't have to deal with the same stumbling blocks that we had to deal with. That's one of the things that's been wrong with our educational system traditionally. We've all been in our silos—whether you were a classroom teacher or a school as a whole, there wasn't a lot of collaboration. But as you know, we wouldn't be talking here today without collaborating. There's such an amazing group of smart people just a push of a button a way. Those people have shared so much with me, I've learned so much from the people in my PLN I sometimes think I don't have any original thoughts. But I too want to share the successes and more so the failures so people don't run into trouble.... If you take one wrong turn as a leader and it was something you could have avoided if you or I would have shared it, then it's actually a failure on our part because we didn't get that out there. We owe it to other educators and the impact it could have on kids down the road.

CH: One last question. Any last-minute advice to a district leader that's just about to embark on a mobile learning initiative?

PL: Make sure that you build a network of three to five educators, like a core group, that you can rely on. It can be more than that, but you want to make it manageable. Build yourself a network of other administrators that are a little ahead of you and stay in communication with them as you go along this journey. The other big thing beyond educating yourself is running community nights. Bring parents in and show them what you are doing. Show them what's happening in other schools. Educate your community as to why this is so important and what your kids will be able to do. Just like I mentioned earlier about me learning from kids, parents seeing their kids with devices in school is a foreign concept. We need to show them that it's not wasted screen time. You can make your community a lot smarter in the whole digital learning experience by having these open conversations and letting them ask questions. Even something as simple as parents helping other parents on how they deal with devices at the home. Some parents might have some good strategies that will help other parents that are struggling with this at home. So, really, those are the two things. I know you asked for one but you get a bonus. (laughs)

CH: All right, bonus!

PL: Build yourself a network and connect with your community and have frequent meetings with them to dispel myths and help them learn as well.

CH: That is great advice. He is Patrick Larkin from Burlington Public Schools in Massachusetts. The Assistant Superintendent for Learning and Awesomeness. I'll add to your title.

PL: Aw, thanks, Carl. I can put that on the business card.

CH: Thank you!

Link to the full video interview here:
www.youtube.com/watch?v=Yk9rVUJdsQ8

CHAPTER 4

END GOALS, DIPS, AND UNEXPECTED OUTCOMES

I n our top 10 things not to do as a leader of a mobile device initiative, one item is not to measure effectiveness of an initiative simply by checking test scores. You'll have your share of community members asking for this data, but realize that test scores tied to technology use are fairly ambiguous. Instead, focus on items that you can control and clearly outline your end goals to all stakeholders.

Remember that student learning is the most important objective and that learning can encompass a lot more than a short-term gain in a few test scores. We should be measuring the growth of the "whole student," and that means more than academic measurements. Although students are the primary focus, don't forget all the ancillary purposes and goals of a mobile device initiative. Some of these may vary in scale, but all should be considered when thinking of end goals for your initiatives. Also, be prepared for the inevitable "dip," when it feels as if you are standing in the middle of chaos. Keeping these end goals at the forefront of your mind will help guide you through those stages as well.

Preparing Students for the 21st-century Workplace

The title of this section is a phrase full of buzzwords, but this phrase actually has a lot of merit when plunging into a mobile device initiative. What does the world look like outside of the classroom walls? Do society and the changes in society mirror what is happening in schools?

In 2007, Steve Jobs introduced the iPhone, and the world has never been the same since. We now carry these amazing mobile computers and multimedia studios in our pockets. Yet, no matter how great that innovation was, in the coming decades our own children will look back on smartphones and think of them in much the same way we think of the Commodore 64 or Tandy 1000. What we as adults consider innovative can quickly transition to operational in the blink of an eye.

My youngest daughter, Caroline, will graduate from high school in the year 2031. Let's consider for a moment what she will find when she walks out the doors of that high school. What will be the same? What will be different?

When I ask these questions to a group of parents or teachers, I get the usual responses.

"We'll have flying skateboards" or "3D printers will be everywhere." They all agree that the world will be not only slightly different but *very* different than it is today. However, when I ask those same teachers or parents what they will do differently to anticipate this change, many look perplexed and say, "You mean I can't just keep teaching the same way I have been for the past 25 years in a row?" Or they say, "Do you mean I have to actually adjust my parenting techniques from what my parents passed down to me?"

Indeed, the 21st century requires a new way of thinking.

Making Communication More Efficient

One of the biggest pieces of early feedback we got in our 1:1 was how much more efficient and instantaneous communication had become. When we surveyed our pilot teachers, 96.8% of them pointed out that communication with students had been moderately to greatly improved (see Figure 4.1).

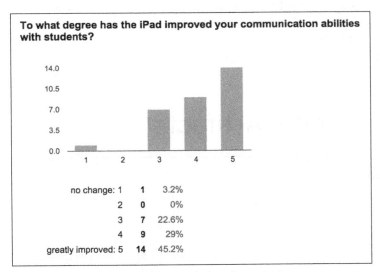

Figure 4.1 Just one survey taker reported no change in degree of communication with students. See the entire survey here: http://tinyurl.com/qyvdtkh.

Students reported similar findings. I remember vividly one student recounting a tale of his previous year without iPads. He told me that in the previous year, if he had an issue with an assignment or a question, it meant he either went home and sat down to email the teacher and then hoped that the teacher would sit down and check their email on their school desktop (if they were working late) or maybe that night when they got home. In some cases the student would get lucky and the teacher might check after school. In other cases, the teacher wouldn't check until morning, generally too late for the student to make improvements or adjust a project.

Once every student *and* every teacher had a mobile device with quick access to email, it meant that waiting and possibly wasting time had diminished. That same student recounted to me that he had an issue in his third period science class. As he headed to lunch, he composed a message to his teacher outlining the issue. By the time lunch had ended, his teacher had responded (likely during her lunch as well), and the student was able to immediately work on improvements to the assignment.

Even those who could not afford access to a personal device were able to communicate as easily as anyone in school. The 1:1 initiative put everyone on the same playing field with the same device and same tools, instantly making communication more effective and efficient.

Creating Digital Artifacts

In the traditional days of school, a student would create a project or great paper and it would end up on the refrigerator for Mom and Dad to see. That meant that not only was the student publishing to an audience of three people (including the teacher), but also their work would have a shelf life equal to its time on the fridge.

Enter in the world of digital devices. Now all students have an opportunity not only to publish to a global audience, but also to give these "artifacts of learning" an unlimited shelf life in digital format.

One of my favorite examples of this is the iBook *The Life of an Eanes Pioneer Child* (Figure 4.2). We are lucky enough to have what is believed to be the oldest schoolhouse in the state of Texas at Eanes Elementary. While this schoolhouse is now a historical site at the back of the actual campus, it is a favorite place for students and teachers to reflect on times before the internet and even electricity. While generations of students have done projects, written papers, and made artifacts around the history of this place, a teacher named Laura Wright (@wrightsbatclass) had a thought. Laura was the first elementary teacher to pilot a 1:1 iPad classroom in our district and realized quickly the power these devices held when it came to content creation. In 2013, her class set out to digitally archive the learning experiences around this historical place.

Figure 4.2 *The Life of an Eanes Pioneer Child* is available for download from iTunes. (http://tinyurl.com/mhgd7re)

Each student in her third grade class was given a chapter to catalog what life was like for kids back in the early 1800s. Now, armed with tools that could let them do more than the written word, students created music, inserted audio narratives, acted out parts, modeled for photos and created poetry around this day and age. One of my favorite chapters is the one on child chores. The fact that kids had to change a chamber pot really resonated with the kids of today and how easy they have it.

All of this made for a much more enriching learning experience than just writing a plain old paper about life in the 1800s, but also, by being digital and actually being published to the iBooks store, a global audience could now experience their work. Students from as far across the world as Turkey responded to their book and the experiences the students had shared. This also meant that at the age of 8, these students were now published authors with work that will stick with them for life.

Increasing Engagement and Motivation to Learn

One could argue that it's hard to learn anything if you aren't motivated and engaged. One of my early encounters with a parent focused on the effect of technology and test scores came right as our pilot was expanding. We had received some great early survey data, particularly around the topics of engagement and motivation, but this particular parent was most concerned with increasing test scores. In one mildly heated exchange at a booster club meeting, he challenged me to come up with hard evidence that this improves test scores. My response: "What if I told you that your child will be more motivated? More engaged? Would that interest you?"

While this surely wasn't the answer he was hoping for, he did have an open mind for that concept and conceded that, if used effectively, this technology might just work out. Indeed, much of the data we collected pointed to just that. In fact, over a three-year period, students reported moderate to significant increases in engagement that ranged from 80.9% to 87.2%. Perhaps even more powerful was the fact that when students were asked to rate the statement "The iPad has enhanced my overall learning experience," the range of students reporting moderate to significant enhancement ranged from 83.5% to 87.9% (Figure 4.3)

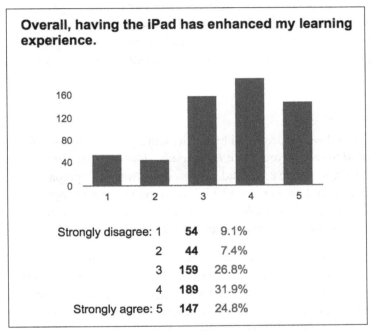

Overall, having the iPad has enhanced my learning experience.

Strongly disagree: 1	**54**	9.1%
2	**44**	7.4%
3	**159**	26.8%
4	**189**	31.9%
Strongly agree: 5	**147**	24.8%

Figure 4.3 Survey results showed that most students felt the iPad enhanced their learning.

Let Risk Taking and the Entrepreneurial Spirit Take Over

While creating digital artifacts and increasing engagement are some great goals to have, there are also some untended things that can happen when you start to put devices in the hands of every student. Dr. Ruben Puentadura refers to the highest level of transformative learning as "redefinition," or the "R" on his SAMR model (http://tinyurl.com/p26mtmv).

Redefinition, according to Puentedura, is when the technology allows for the creation of new tasks that were previously inconceivable. This may not and likely doesn't happen in the classroom every day, but having now experienced a few years of every student with a device in their hands, it happens much more frequently than it did before. Here are two of my favorite examples of redefinition happening in our schools at both an elementary level and a high school level.

Lemonade for Dylan

In the spring of 2013, I was approached by an elementary school parent. She started with "I need to talk to you about *these iPads*." Having gone through several parent meetings, phone calls, and discussions, I was fully prepared to hear a horror story about how her child had done something inappropriate on the device. The emphasis *"these iPads"* even makes it sound as if they are some sort of bad influence from the wrong side of the tracks.

However, I was not only surprised by what happened next, it affected my life going forward. She shared with me the story of her fourth grade daughter (for the sake of this story, we'll call her "Clara"). Clara had a 2-year-old nephew named Dylan who suffered from a rare neurodegenerative disorder known as Krabbe's disease. Although the disease is ultimately fatal, Clara wanted to do something to help her nephew.

So she did what any 10-year-old does who is trying to raise money: She started a lemonade stand. Although she was able to collect $50 or $60 with the lemonade stand, she just felt it wasn't enough. She asked her mom if she could build a website to help raise more money for Dylan and the organization "Hunter's Hope" (http://huntershope.org), a foundation established to address the acute need for information and research about this rare condition. Her mom told her about their uncle who was a web developer, but before she could even finish her sentence, Clara interrupted with "No, Mom—I want to make the site myself." She went on to explain that during the school year, students in her fourth grade classroom had used their iPads and a website-building tool called Weebly to build their own websites. She wanted to design the site and use it to not only raise money for Dylan but also to coordinate other lemonade stands around the city.

I was floored. At the age of 10 this student not only used technology in a way to further her cause, she also was a project manager and planner for organizing lemonade stands all over the city. While Dylan would ultimately pass away in 2014, his hope and spirit are carried on by all those affected by his story and the story shared by his extremely motivated 10-year-old aunt. Powerful! Here is a link to the website: http://lemonadefordylan.weebly.com.

Is There an App for That?

In the fall of 2013, sophomore Michael Bartmess faced a challenge. He was taking American Sign Language (ASL) and needed help practicing his finger spelling. Thinking on his feet, he quickly perused the App Store in hopes of finding some sort of tool to help him with this skill.

He was disappointed to learn that there really weren't any great options out there for him. However, he had an idea. He had just completed his first year of iOS coding and thought this would be a great opportunity to create an app to help not only him, but his fellow students. So, during the summer of 2013, that's exactly what he set out to do. He worked with several "hand models" and a graphic designer student to create the "ASL Finger-Spell" app (see Figure 4.4), and it is currently available for free in the app store.

He also worked with his ASL class to give him feedback on version 1 and help with improvements that he would later release in version 1.2. Now more than 3,000 people have downloaded the app to help them with finger spelling more than 5,000 words. For more on the story, check out Lisa Johnson's (@techchef4U) post here: (http://tinyurl.com/oju8or5)

While both of these stories speak just as much to the motivation and internal drive of the specific students, without the access to technology, these outcomes would not have been possible, or at the very least, they would be highly unlikely. All of this to say you never know what kind of unintended "redefined" learning can happen without first providing that level of access.

iTunes Preview

ASL Finger-Spelling

By Michael Bartmess

Open iTunes to buy and download apps.

Description

Finger-Spelling provides a fantastic and conveni...
control over the length of words and the speed, ...

ASL Finger-Spelling Support ›

What's New in Version 1.2.1

Version 1.2.1
-Fixes crash on startup

View in iTunes

Free

Category: Education
Updated: Nov 27, 2013

Figure 4.4 The ASL Finger-Spelling app provides control over the length of words and the pace of practice. (http://tinyurl.com/ngex2lt)

Experiencing "the Dip"

In Michael Fullan's paper "Leading in a Culture of Change," he mentions something called the Implementation Dip. "The implementation dip is literally a dip in performance and confidence as one encounters an innovation that requires new skills and new understandings" (Fullan, 2001; http://tinyurl.com/nfkw3cd). Fullan goes on to point out that all successful schools will experience this dip at some point during their journey toward innovation.

Our goal should be to make the dip as shallow as possible and not last more than a few days or weeks. When we began our WiFi pilot in 2011, we experienced a brief dip early with our 1:1. It was commonplace early on to see students in the back of class looking at the teacher while at the same time gently tilting their iPad from side to side (obviously playing some sort of game). Distraction can be a challenge when students hold a wealth of information in their hands, and this is especially true in traditional "lecture-style" classrooms where the teacher is supposed to be the sole source of information. We found that in classrooms where students were engaged and empowered to drive their learning, the distraction level was nearly gone. However, teachers are human, and they take time to change their practices and strategies, too.

While I thought that early dip was interesting, the beauty and joy of rolling out a mobile device initiative in phases is that you get to experience the dip over and over again! Kind of like your own personal roller coaster of expectations and outcomes, only not quite as much fun. In the fall of 2012, I remember the exact moment we entered into the bottom of an implementation dip.

We had just finished one of our parent night presentations for middle school and high school parents. This was about one month after every eighth grade student had received their iPad and taken them home. At the end of the meeting, I was surrounded by a "mob" of angry parents. They were frustrated with this new disruption in their homes, and as the person leading this initiative, I was the perfect target to receive their frustration.

As the dozen or so parents surrounded me, I noticed my superintendent walking out the back door and mouthing the words to me, "You've got this." I couldn't help but smile. While the finger-pointing and raised voices continued to increase, my smile widened. I had just hit the rock bottom point of the dip, and my smile was because I knew that the only way we could go from here was up.

Then a parent angrily asked, "Why are you smiling? We're mad at you!" I looked at all the parents and said, "I'm smiling because we are having this conversation/argument now. While I know it's uncomfortable and uneasy, the fact that we are talking about this now means that we can affect the outcomes of your child's digital life now rather than hope for the best when they leave your home after high school." While that didn't satisfy all the parents, the message had been heard. And for me and our district, it meant it was time to begin the climb out of the dip toward the mountain of success.

Unexpected Outcomes

I mentioned the unintended outcomes created by the students, but one of the other unexpected things that happened that makes taxpayers happy is the amount of money saved by "obsoleting" certain technologies. Before the 1:1 iPads, Eanes ISD purchased many technology items that performed different functions to facilitate learning in the classroom. Whether it be a wireless slate to control the classroom computer or a cassette recorder to record students' reading, the following items in Table 4.1 represent a list of technology purchased by the district before the LEAP Initiative. Most of the items, unless otherwise noted, were purchased for every classroom. One major advantage of an iPad 1:1 is that now all of these items are replaced with free or inexpensive apps with access for every student.

Some other items that we see trending toward obsolescence because of 1:1 include:

- **Dictionaries.** The state still requires us to purchase these.

- **TI-84 calculator.** We are piloting its replacement with the free Desmos app.

- **Textbooks.** Ebooks are often less expensive.

- **Paper.** The use of this resource continues to decrease with the integration of iPads, Google tools, and Learning Management Systems.

Although making these items obsolete was not part of our initiative's goals, it does show you how much things can change when you give every student a device. These are unexpected outcomes that we all can appreciate, especially those who are financially supporting technology use in your schools.

Table 4.1

Previously purchased technology and the iPads/apps that replaced them.

PREVIOUSLY PURCHASED ITEM	REPLACEMENT ON IPAD
Digital camera ($150—one per grade level and a class set per campus)	Camera app (free)
Document camera ($600)	Camera app (free)
SMART Slate or AirLiner ($300)	Splashtop app ($4.99)
Student response systems ($1500 class set)	Socrative (free), Kahoot (free) Nearpod (free)
Video camera ($250) + editing software ($99)	Camera app (free) + iMovie app (free)
DVD/VHS player ($100)	Video app (free) YouTube (free) MediaCore ($2/student)
CD players ($75)	iTunes Music app (Free)
Atlas, globe, classroom map ($25)	Map app (free) Google Earth (free)
Microsoft Office licenses ($75 per computer)	Microsoft Office suite of apps (free) iWork suite of apps (free)
Thesaurus ($22)	Thesaurus app (free) Built-in thesaurus (free)
Polycom Video Conference System ($2000)	Facetime app (free)
Scanner ($75)	JotNot app (free) or Genius Scanner app (free)
Cassette recorder system ($150) iPod/MP3 recorder ($100)	GarageBand app (free) AudioNote app ($4.99)
Kurzweil screen reading software/hardware ($995—for special education)	Dragon Dictation app (free) Built-in iOS feature

CHAPTER 5

BUILDING A BRAND

Eric Sheninger (@E_Sheninger) says, "If you don't tell your story, someone else will for you." This is especially true in the case of a mobile device initiative. One needs to look no further than the case of LAUSD and their botched iPad initiative as a case where their story was crafted for them. While the district may have put out a press release when it started their initiative, it did little else to really "sell the why" behind what they were doing.

During this chapter, we'll look at some famous brands around the world and how we can use their models of success to help with leading a mobile device initiative. After looking at those global brands, we'll dive into how to create an effective logo or message around your initiative and explore strategies for marketing it effectively. We'll look at the importance of having a common language among staff and how best to share your story with your community. Last, we'll investigate ways to expand, grow, and evolve your brand as your initiative evolves.

Global Brands

To be a successful company, you must have a brand or image that transcends the regular marketplace. A company's ability to be known or recognized can sometimes teeter just on the name alone. While these companies all have multi-million-dollar marketing firms and we do not, we can still learn from their tactics and employ some of these same strategies in our mobile learning brand.

Apple

Apple Inc. is probably one of the best companies in the world at "selling the why." As Simon Sinek mentions in his TED Talk on the golden circle, Apple sells you on the lifestyle and the image, not so much the technology behind it. Watching their ads and seeing their signature glowing Apple on the backs of laptops in shows and movies makes you feel like whoever uses their product is cool, efficient, and creative. Selling the "why" is an important part of your own branding.

Coca-Cola

We all know soda is bad for us, right? Have you ever poured Coke on a car battery and watched it become magically clean? Do you want to pour that into your body? Yet, somehow, we all want to drink it. Much like Apple, the Coca-Cola brand and advertising is placed just about everywhere you look, and they sell you on the coolness and hipness of drinking their product. One other thing they seem to do really well is effectively integrate the local culture to sell their products.

McDonald's

Arguably one of the world's most recognizable symbols, McDonald's (like Coca-Cola) has succeeded despite the fact that they make unhealthy foods quickly. One thing about McDonald's and it's advertisements is the fact that they are adaptable to change. Look at some of their recent ads and you'll see more and more about salads, fruit, and the lack of trans fat. While they have a stalwart of a brand, they don't rest on their laurels. They respond to their customers and adapt to make their product and brand better. This is definitely something to consider when laying out your mobile learning brand.

Nike

Home to one of the most famous motto's of all time ("Just Do it"), Nike is expensive, over-priced athletic footwear, and apparel that *everyone* must own. Wearing their shoes makes you feel not only like a hip athlete, but also like one with sole (get it?). Although Nike has received bad press about child-labor issues, the company was able to overcome all of that with a marketing campaign that never quits. It's hard to hear the whispers when Nike is shouting.

Create a Logo and Name for Your Brand

So we have seen that having a striking image (such as Nike's swoosh or Apple's bitten apple) carries a lot of weight in the world. Although we don't have multi-million-dollar marketing firms at our disposal, we can use their strategy to our advantage. Think of what symbols we commonly use around education and technology. Some of the images in Figure 5.1 are symbols I have seen schools use for mobile learning initiatives.

Figure 5.1 You could use these images to symbolize technology initiatives.

I threw the antiquated diskette in there just to see if you were paying attention, but you get the drift. These could represent "EmPOWERing Learning" or "Downloading Knowledge," but the idea is having a noticeable symbol that subtly suggests that technology is a part of this, but not necessarily the main part. Remember—it's all about the learning.

Creating a common word or phrase for everyone to get behind is an important step in launching an initiative. In our initial pilot at Westlake high school, we had the "WiFi" Pilot in which WiFi stood for Westlake Initiative For Innovation. This tagline worked well for us as a logo (Figure 5.2) because it conveyed the message of innovation and made for an easy acronym to refer to whenever discussing the pilot program. Without that, the initiative would have just become the "iPad Pilot," which may not seem like a big deal, but I'll go into greater detail in a minute about why that simple change in nomenclature can make a big difference down the road. When it comes to naming your initiative, try to either use a common name in your district or an acronym that will incorporate what you are doing in a clever way. We started with our WiFi program in 2011, as the program hadn't gone districtwide yet. One of our middle schools did something similar with it's C5 Initiative, which stood for "Connect, Create, Communicate, Collaborate, Cougars" (their mascot is a Cougar). Eventually we would settle on "LEAP" (Learning & Engaging through Access and Personalization) as our acronym of choice.

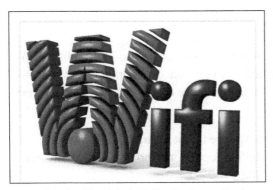

Figure 5.2 Our Westlake Initiative For Innovation logo.

Regardless of a clever name or acronym, you'll want to be careful not to tie it too closely with a device or piece of technology. I've seen some like "iLearn" or "Chromebooks for ED" that hint or directly mention a device. By putting a device in the title of your initiative's logo, you've instantly made sure that logo will become obsolete at some point. Technology changes so rapidly that including a name of a device instead of a more abstract idea closes down your options for the future. In the year or two before iPads, the netbook revolution seemed to be taking over. If you decided to take on one-to-one netbooks and gave it the brand "NetBooks & U" or "N.E.S.T." (Netbooks Engaging Students with Technology), all of a sudden you have completely committed to that single piece of hardware. When 2010 rolled around and the world of learning became more available via the tablet, initiatives that used the word *laptop* in their name felt outdated. They were essentially handcuffed to a particular tool.

Also, any educational program should be about the learning (I think I've said that a few times now, haven't I?), so centering the title around a device wouldn't really send that message. Keep students and learning as your focus and a hint of technology in your logo and the message will be clear: Learning is important, and this technology will help that.

Have a Strategy

If you've done all the legwork and marketing research around establishing a powerful brand, don't waste it by failing to execute on the message. While we may not have million-dollar marketing firms, we do have access to some very creative students and staff.

Have a logo design contest and leverage the talent around you to create a memorable image. That alone also tells a good story and message about integrating student talent into your initiative.

Before you go further, you should also try and grab a few "things." Check for the domain name around your brand and see what social media accounts are out there. While you'll want this tied to the school district, you'll want it also to be it's own go-to source for information. The domain for "LEAP" was taken, but we did make sure that all important information was funneled through our district website page dedicated to the initiative at http://eanesisd.net/leap.

When we eventually launched our learning festival, called iPadpalooza, and our iLeap Academy, we didn't make that same mistake and quickly grabbed both iPadpalooza.com and iLeapAcademy.com, as well as Facebook pages, twitter, Instagram, YouTube, and Google+ accounts. Even if you have no current plan for using these, it makes sense to grab them early—the potential use down the road makes it worth the 5 minutes it takes to set up an account.

Whenever you send out any messages around the initiative, be sure to always include the brand/logo and a link back to the main site. You always want to covertly push people back to your brand in order to have both consistent messaging and, as we'll talk about in the next section, a common language.

Common Language and Procedures

In a school district you have administrators, teachers, secretaries, bus drivers, students, parents, and a bevy of other people tied to your learning community. Having all of them speak the same language is a huge step in having success around your initiative. For example, if you have a new student enter the district and they are given this device on day one, what are the expectations for that student? How are they trained, and who will relay these expectations? Having everyone on the same page means that students, teachers, counselors, and administrators who come into contact with the new student all speak the same language and can put the student on the right path.

One area where we failed early on was having these students fall through the cracks, which in turn meant that their parents were kept in the dark. Teachers didn't have any established procedures or common language for handling new students when it came to getting them established and set up on their device. The whole system was falling apart, except for the fact that we had an educational technology point person at every campus. Without that main contact person, many of these students would be running around aimlessly.

Admittedly, having that single point person saves us in many ways when it comes to just-in-time learning, deployment strategies, app purchasing, provisioning, and so forth. Because most districts don't have those people on staff, it becomes even more important to have a common language, expectation, and procedure around your initiative.

Evolve and Share the Brand

Once the brand around your initiative has been established, it's easy to sit back and rest on your laurels as things progress. The truth is your brand should be ever evolving and expanding. Our initiative went through one major brand overhaul from "WiFi Project" to "LEAP Initiative," but we've since used the branding and success around LEAP to expand it to include more than just the initiative.

One of the best examples of this is our recent success with our iLeap Academy. (http://tinyurl.com/olg4l4f). The basis for the academy is having others learn from our mistakes and also see 1:1 in action. While we have had many districts come for site visits since the early going, it was hard to really teach them all the things that they should be aware of in a mobile device initiative. Enter iLeap Academy (Figure 5.3).

Figure 5.3 Our logo for iLeap Acadamy.

Having both attended and delivered professional learning for staff around mobile devices, my ed-tech team and myself started to notice a trend. Whenever you see or hear about these initiatives, it's usually at a conference where all you can really do is show videos or photos of 1:1 in action. Conversely, when people come to see your 1:1 in action in a site visit, they get to see it, but rarely learn the backstory or how to apply the same strategies we did for success. The iLeap Academy was a mashup of these two concepts, and by hosting it in our own district, we were able not only to expand the brand of LEAP and Eanes, but also to provide unique learning experiences for our attendees (Figure 5.4).

In addition to brand expansion, these academies provided revenue that was not from the taxpayers. This meant we now had additional resources for funding innovation projects and risk-taking ideas.

One other unexpected outcome came from our own teachers who participated in the academy as "iLeap Mentors." These teachers created lesson templates, came in after school to be part of a panel, and let guests enter their classroom for three days in a row to see an technology-infused learning project in its various stages. As part of being a mentor, they were given a stipend for their time. Although money isn't much of a motivating factor for most in education, it was a nice way to say thanks for the dedication to improving and evolving their craft and letting others experience it. As other teachers have gotten wind of this, there is now an uptick in enthusiasm around staff wanting to be a mentor in the future.

You'll have ups and downs and moments of stagnation with your initiative. Besides the implementation dips I mentioned in Chapter 4, there will also be times where the enthusiasm has drifted and the nuance has worn off. Having an event like this to reinvigorate your staff and expand your brand is a powerful step in sustaining the program for years to come.

Figure 5.4 iLeap attendees watching our 1:1 program in action.

CHAPTER 6

CREATING A CULTURE OF INNOVATION

No one likes failure, least of all schools. The institution of public education is built around the concept that students pass certain standards to move on to the next level. An environment centered around passing and avoiding failure isn't really conducive to risk-taking. Yet, when I go out and listen to various entrepreneurs speak, they consistently mention the fact that you have to be willing to take risks.

I've also noticed an exponential trend in schools being asked to "celebrate" failure as a step in the learning process. While I love this positive approach, leaders tend to struggle with this concept when it comes to their own learning. Although they are not elected officials, school leaders such as superintendents have to answer to both the state and their school board when it comes making decisions. Taking risks and failing (a definite possibility based on the fact you are taking a risk) carry some consequences—mainly that you could lose your job.

Being a teacher in a classroom can be one of the most humbling professions out there. Teachers aren't allowed to have huge egos because their students, the parents, or other staff will quickly sniff that out and squash it. However, the further removed from the classroom an educator is, the more the ego begins to swell. I experienced this firsthand moving from being a classroom teacher to teaching computer lab. While I still worked with children, I no longer had to deal with parents or grades. As I've moved through the ranks in my district positions, I've found that the higher I go, the bigger the egos become.

Don't get me wrong—having an ego isn't a bad thing when it comes to leadership. You need to be confident in your actions and decisive when it comes to handling conflicts. The downside to having a large ego is the fear of taking risks or failure. One doesn't become a leader (and by proxy successful) by messing up all the time. Looking back in history, you can find many great leaders who became great after they took great risks.

It might have been easier for Rosa Parks to sit in the back of the bus and follow the rules, but she decided to take a risk. Steve Jobs could have spurned Apple and stuck with his side businesses because of a grudge or negative attitude, but instead he saw his return as a tremendous opportunity. Many of our great leaders took risks and made sometimes seemingly illogical choices at the time to accomplish great things.

Part of being a leader in a mobile device initiative is creating a mindset and culture around innovation. Innovation by definition is "something new or different introduced; the introduction of new things or methods." It's really hard to be innovative by following the rules. In fact, by definition, people could never be innovative if they did that, because the rules do not represent new things or new methods.

The Marshmallow Challenge: Putting Innovation to the Test

One of my favorite activities to do with a group of superintendents is the marshmallow challenge. This is a design challenge popularized by a Tom Wujec TED talk. The idea is simple. You and your team have 18 minutes to create the tallest free-standing structure that can sustain the weight of a single marshmallow on top. You are limited in scope by the tools with which you can build (20 sticks of spaghetti, a yard of tape, a yard of string) and by the limited time you have to complete the task (18 minutes).

Having directed this challenge to a wide variety of audiences, I'm always most intrigued by how superintendents and district leaders do. The truth is, they consistently perform worse than teachers or students. Why is that? The main reasons go back to the points at the beginning of this chapter. While all of the leaders in the room have a high level of competitiveness, they also have a high level of ego. With only 18 minutes to create a tall structure, there is usually a little jockeying for power at the onset. Then there is usually some level of discussion. A committee is then planned to talk about when the next committee should meet. Plans are drawn and finally voted on, at which point there are about 5 minutes left. Frantically, the leaders go into crisis mode (a surefire way to kill creativity) and usually just start maniacally sticking pieces of spaghetti together with tape. In the end, the results are always the same: the marshmallow does not remain at the top.

This challenge is a microcosm of the culture in your school and the mindset of administration—creating unnecessary meetings, arguing points of theory, but never actually applying the theories until it's too late. This kind of thing happens in schools all the time. We have great plans and ideas, but rarely take action on them until it becomes a crisis.

Teams of school leaders that generally perform the best on this challenge are teams that regularly try and break the rules, teams that work well together quickly, teams that use the internet to "borrow" some examples, and teams willing to steal other teams' best ideas. While breaking rules and cheating don't sound like the "right" way to win, it generally means that leaders in those groups aren't bound by normal structures and strategies. They are willing to bend some rules and think creatively about the task at hand and therefore become far more successful and innovative in their solutions.

For more information about running one of these challenges, check out The Marshmallow Challenge at http://marshmallowchallenge.com.

Modeling Risk Taking: #NoEmail4Lent

In the fall of 2012, I emailed the students of Westlake High School to ask them for feedback on a certain app. I then proceeded to wait for two solid weeks before one of the 2,600 students wrote me back. I had a mixture of emotions when I got that one email, so I decided to follow up with another question. "I'm so happy you emailed me, but why didn't any other students write me back?" His answer was both simple and profound: "We don't do email."

I was floored.

What do you mean you don't "do" email? Despite being flummoxed by the response, I decided to take this as a learning opportunity. If today's students don't communicate with just email, what tools do they use? As a director of "innovation" I felt strangely un-innovative and out of touch with the youth of today. How could I learn their tools for communication and totally immerse myself in it? The answer would appear a few short months later when my wife asked me what I was going to give up for Lent.

I decided that would be the perfect time frame to go off of email and try all these other new tools. So in the spring of 2013, if you sent me an email any time after February 12, you would get the auto-response found in Figure 6.1.

```
Hi -
I'm in the office, but have given up email for Lent -

To contact me please try one of the following methods:
(from easiest to hardest)

 1. Chat (via gmail) - chooker@eanesisd.net account
 2. Text - 512-537-7015
 3. Direct message or Tweet via Twitter - @mrhooker
 4. Face to face conversation
 5. Dispatch.io - Invite chooker@eanesisd.net to a dispatch
 6. Google+ - http://goo.gl/OqxbT
 7. LinkedIN - http://lnkd.in/sHb4BJ
 8. Office phone - 512-732-9020 |
 9. Voicemail (via Google Voice) - 512-537-7015
10. Facebook - http://www.facebook.com/eisd.carlhooker
11. Edmodo - http://50.edmodo.com/profile/1947250
12. My blog - http://hookedoninnovation.com/contact
13. Skype - username: MrHooker
14. TCEA Social Community: http://tcea.mymemberfuse.com/
15. Mail a letter to my office - 601 Camp Craft Rd, Austin, TX 78746
```

Figure 6.1 The 15 other communication channels I offered to students and staff.

Although I thought having all these multiple forms of communication would make it easier to communicate, in fact it made it much harder. By removing the main stream of communication and only using side channels, I found myself missing large (and important) pieces of information when it came to district decisions. So, after 19 days of going without email, I opened up my inbox and quickly started back-tracking all the conversations I had missed.

Despite not making it the entire 40 days, there were some other outcomes I discovered. I had hoped that I'd be able to do "more meaningful" work while not checking email. While I did get quite a few more personal chores done in the evening, work seemed largely unaffected. It seems much of my "meaningful work" came from the sometimes mundane tasks assigned to me via email. I feel like this wasn't as much of a success, largely because I had to spend more time checking all the various methods of communication.

My other hope was that not sitting behind my screen as much would force more face-to-face communication and collaboration. I can say without a doubt: That was the greatest success of this experiment. I spent more time with my family, talked to district staff I hadn't seen in a while, and even got to sub in a first grade classroom! While this seems like a simple idea, I was amazed at how touched people were by this concept of walking away from email to spend more time with others. I even had a small group of people (in admin no less) suggest we have an "unEmail Day" once a month to get out and see the kids, campuses, and staff. This will be something I employ going forward every month.

The last of the outcomes I hoped for was that I would have others communicate in different ways. Aside from a few folks that were stuck on email as the only method of communication, I felt this was a success as well. I had a principal join Twitter and a GT teacher chat with me via Edmodo (www.edmodo.com), and I got to chat with someone face to face (virtually) via Skype rather than a back-and-forth email exchange. I even had one parent communicate with me using smoke signals (they were smoking brisket in their backyard). I also finally got myself on Instagram (@Hookertech), since that seems to be a preferred communication method among kids. Although the only letter I got was a printed-off email, I really feel like making others aware of the alternative methods, and the way kids communicate put things in perspective for most.

So while this very large risk failed, it also succeeded, because not only did it influence my own personal behavior going forward, it made others much more thoughtful about their interactions. As a leader trying to build this culture of innovation, taking risks with a set of expectations and outcomes is important. Documenting those outcomes and then sharing the success or failure is important if others are to learn from it, but also set a tone that trying something and failing, if well thought out, isn't a bad thing.

Failing Out Loud

When a company or individual fails, it's plastered all over the internet. In some ways, people are unfairly judged by the missteps or failures. In other ways, we hold certain individuals (such as celebrities and athletes) to a higher set of standards than we do for ourselves. So when public figures fail, we have a tendency to shame them if for no other reason than to make ourselves feel better.

School districts have taken a beating over the years from media and legislators taking isolated examples of failure in a school and then painting the rest of education with a broad brush of similar failure. An administrator cheats on a high-stakes test, or a teacher says something inappropriate on social media, and the story reaches the four corners of the universe. Never mind that when billionaires cheat to gain an edge, they're seen as innovative (unless they are arrested, in which case they get a golden parachute). Celebrities who are outspoken on social media generally increase their status and number of followers. Teachers who are outspoken on social media generally decreases their status of employment and number of paychecks.

So with this inherent injustice already in place with American media, why would any leader or educator take a risk? Worse yet, if the risk fails, why would you want anyone to know about it? I think we have been running in fear of speaking the truth. When we take risks and attempt things for the betterment of a child's education, this shouldn't be something to be shamed for, it should be applauded. Too often in districts we try to display a rose-colored image of what perfection looks like rather than showing the realities of failure that took place to get there.

Many of my "Top 10 Things Not to Do" lists are a direct result of taking the proactive approach and failing "out loud." By doing this, you not only display all your cards, you also share the strategies you have in place to make it better. This means that others can learn from your mistakes and share their own ideas and concepts. By not sharing mistakes, you garner less goodwill and more distrust from your community.

Celebrating Failure

A simple activity that you can do with your staff to celebrate failure is have them try a brain challenge or improvisational activity, and when they mess up, have them hold their hands up high and shout "Woo-hoo!" I learned this practice at an Apple Distinguished Educator event, and it has stuck with me ever since. It makes failing and taking risks a fun thing, and it actually decreases the anxiety level around failure.

Failing out loud as a leader can be a tough concept to grasp, especially if that leader is a control freak, a leader without a lot of self-esteem, or one who lacks self-confidence. One strategy I have used recently with a lot of success is the concept of "PowerPoint Karaoke."

The concept is this: You are given a topic (such as the state of education or technology in the classroom) and then the audience chooses an unrelated noun (such as Fruit Loops or baseball). Using the online app called Pechaflickr (http://pechaflickr.net) you set the number of slides and time of each slide—I like 10 slides in 10 seconds—and plug in the audience word of choice.

Once started, the presenter must then try to tie their presentation to the completely random Flickr images appearing on the screen. Some of these can be fairly basic (depending on the noun chosen) while others can end up being quite hilarious and provocative. I once saw a superintendent who was brave enough to try this in front of his entire faculty. Not only did he pull it off, but when he messed up (or failed), the staff actually cheered him on even louder.

By modeling risk taking and accepting this challenge, even briefly, he set the tone for his staff that taking a risk can be a good thing. He also endeared himself to his staff as he struggled to find the right words for each image that appeared on the screen. They laughed and cried with him, and to this day, I don't know many other superintendents that have the level of support that he has from his staff. Did this all happen because of this silly challenge? No! But, because he set the tone and publicly failed out loud, his staff became much more aware of his attitude and character when it comes to innovation in his district.

The district culture was now set, and as a result, despite being a small district in east Texas, more innovative ideas for student learning are coming from his schools than from any others around him.

Get Out of the Way!

Sometimes the best way to foster innovation, creativity, and risk-taking is to get out of the way and create avenues for your staff to do this. I recently heard a panel of school leaders from innovative districts speak about their mobile device initiatives. When asked about innovative ideas or risk taking, all of them noted that they had a staff member in their district who was the main driving force behind the innovation.

Having an employee drive the initiative allows you to support it both by clearing roadblocks and by showcasing their successes. It shows that you don't have to be the center of attention and focus, and it builds capital with your staff. As we'll see in the next chapter about shared ownership, this type of "flat" leadership can actually encourage more innovation and risk taking in your schools. As long as that innovation is always geared toward improving the learning environment for your students, the risk taking and mini failures that come along the way are merely steps in improving that learning process.

CHAPTER 7

CULTIVATING SHARED OWNERSHIP

Leaders are interested in finding the best way
rather than having their own way.

—JOHN WOODEN

You have a lot of good ideas. You have a lot of bad ones, too. Just because you are given the title of chief or director or superintendent doesn't mean that you have the best ideas. Another quote I like is one from David Weinberger, who says, "The smartest person in the room is the room itself." If you include more minds in the process, you will actually get more ideas and, as a result of having their buy-in, more success.

However, is buy-in the same as ownership? People may believe in what you are doing, but that doesn't necessarily mean they actually feel like part of the decision-making process. No one likes to be told what they are going to do without a chance to offer feedback, especially teachers who have many years of experience under their belt. One of the biggest issues at the university level (besides the bureaucracy) is the fact that tenured professors really don't need to spend time helping kids learn. It's their job to show up and spew knowledge, and it's the students' job to sit there and take notes before the knowledge leaves the room.

In a shared ownership model, students would be helping set course for where they want to sail. Instead, the professor, as "captain" of the classroom, is setting the sails, steering the ship, and sending student's off the plank (during those infamous "weed-out" quizzes). How do we change this behavior?

Steve Jobs is famous for saying, "It doesn't make sense to hire smart people and then tell them what to do; we hire smart people so they can tell us what to do." Google CEOs Larry Page and Sergey Brin have a very similar motto in that they "hire people smarter than we are." Both of these companies share many traits in common, one of them being that they are so successful. They build a culture where everyone is committed to continually improving the company. Employees at these companies feel respected, listened to, and valued for their work and opinion. Enter K–12 education, and the top-down structure is often the norm. It's tough to get buy-in and shared ownership when you are being told (or, worse, not being told) what the expectations are without a chance to provide input or get an explanation. Want to make a mobile device initiative fail? Don't ask for any input and see how far that gets you.

Beating the Evil Villain (aka "the District")

I'm convinced that at some point in my life I'll make a comic book about this. In the comic, there will be a character who swoops in and disrupts things or messes up the classroom. It seems that no matter where you work, inevitably you encounter rumors of this evil villain, known only as "the District." This evildoer also tends to make appearances at faculty meetings after an objective has been handed down. He appears in the back of the faculty lounge following some sort of job or pay cut. But, his favorite place to appear is whenever there is a decision made without any input. Is such a case, the villain would say, "The District decided that we are going to do a 1:1 mobile device initiative." I alluded to this in Chapter 2 when I mentioned hearing a principal saying this. In doing so, he instantly deflated any belief in the initiative itself while at the same time telling his staff subtly that he doesn't have anything to do with the decision. In this case, the District character is handing down mandates while twirling his evil mustache.

"Who decided that we should have late start days this year? Oh, the district." Again, some decision made without buy-in reveals our anti-hero once again at the end of the statement above. People place blame on this fictional third-party character even though they themselves technically are a part of the very thing they blame. Staff who feel they are part of the process and decision making also tend to be more a part of the actual district and thus are less likely to play the blame game.

"Who decided that we should have late start days? Well, actually it was a whole group of teachers and leaders who got together to go over the calendar. *We decided it.*" Suddenly you see the impact of shared ownership and the killing of the supervillain the District. This shared ownership will be vital in the success of your initiative and it will serve as the kryptonite to "the District." Everyone must believe in the "why" and have belief in the mission and goals of the program.

Leading from the Side

As a leader, you want your face to be in front. You didn't get as far as you did by sitting by idly while others did your work, did you? Actually, one of the traits of a great leader is building up the support and strengths of those around you. Promoting the strengths of those on your team or in your district means that you are putting people in places where they can best succeed. You wouldn't hire a great baker and then tell him his job was to refill glasses of water in the restaurant. That's a serious misuse of his talent, yet we do this all the time in education.

I've been lucky enough to work with some amazing and talented people when it comes to educational technology. They all share similar traits in that they want to be creative and work with people, and they will work tirelessly on something they are passionate about. I can also say with almost 100% certainty that not even one of them liked the menial tasks they encountered on a daily basis. Their creativity feels stifled when they have to do some simple data-entry or run a projector/slide show for another person. They could be spending this time creating and collaborating, but instead they are fixing printers and changing projector bulbs.

I relate completely to these people, because I am truly a person who despises mundane, repetitive tasks. I once worked for a technology services department making Windows "images" for machines. This required countless hours pushing the "Next" or "OK" button while a variety of software downloaded on the image. After two days of doing this and not speaking to a single human being, I decided it was time for me to find a new profession.

We focus on hierarchies in education, just as businesses do. However, I've found that practicing the concept of "flat" leadership has had a strong impact on the success of our initiative. In the flat leadership model, there isn't a hierarchy so much as a web of resources. Everyone is on the same page, and anyone can lead a discussion or handle a problem. A big problem with hierarchies is that people "below" the leader tend to feel like they have no power to think or decide on their own and kick issues and ideas up to the top. Rather than being self-sufficient and self-motivated, they feel incapacitated because of their lack of shared ownership. As a result, they are not as likely to share ideas. I'll admit that I still have a hard time surrendering control and giving up the notion that every idea must be my own, but when I've stepped aside and let the team lead, amazing and innovative things have happened.

Hire People with Skills and Vision

Of course, one of the things that makes flat leadership and shared ownership most successful is when you hire people who are best suited for that environment. When it comes time to hire a new employee, I try to follow the lead of the innovative companies I mentioned before, such as Google and Apple. Trying to find a person who shares the vision of the district but also one who fits the strengths of the others is important.

However, our typical interview process in public schools is full of holes. It is antiquated and proprietary, and it lends itself to the traditional hierarchical model, not to one of shared ownership. In the fall of 2012, I changed that process into something that not only got us the best candidate, but also supported the notion of shared ownership.

Going through the interview process can be time-consuming and cumbersome, so I wanted to make sure that we had the following:

- Ample time to accept qualified candidates

- A group of core staff who filtered the applications with a rating system

- A component that allowed us to have a "sneak preview" of potential candidates and a component that gave candidates an opportunity to highlight their creativity

- A smaller group of core staff to interview those who made it through the application process

- A larger group of core staff actually being trained by the finalists in a professional development setting

It's those last three components that I'd really like to focus on. Individuals don't always show what they truly are like on paper or in an interview setting. I've often said that when it comes to the presidential election, we should put all the candidates on an island, a Survivor-style TV show, and see who makes it. Those of us at home will see the true colors of the candidates.

Since we didn't have a television show or an island, I decided to use technology to help us (see my chapter on modeling) and actually use tech tools to help us figure out personalities. So, as candidates are deemed "qualified" by our initial application rating system, they are given one week to create a video of two minutes or less about themselves that highlights their strengths and what they could bring to our team. Some took this as an opportunity to create innovative videos showcasing their talents, while others just sat in front of a webcam and talked for their two minutes. Doing this meant that our team could see a large array of candidates in a short amount of time rather than spending hours interviewing each one.

The next big part of this process was the mock training component—only there was nothing mock about this training. It represented the final step in a lengthy, elaborate process. Those making it to this final round were all extremely talented and worthy of the position. However, seeing them in action in what would be their actual setting was not only eye opening, but also extremely informative as to how they work, operate, and relate.

Although this process has yielded some tremendous employees and members of my team, the interesting part is that it also involved more than 20 people from all different levels over the course of a month. Everyone was invested in the success of these new employees, as they had played a major role in them being hired.

When You Are the Problem

Sometimes we tend to be our own worst enemy. I tend to have a vision for how I want something to turn out and feel that I'm the only one who can execute an idea that way. Early on in my career and during this initiative, I didn't trust anyone else to handle the delivery of a message or the communication of the vision. This made the vision very narrow-sighted and didn't make others really feel much interest in supporting it.

It's perhaps ironic that it took a student project to make me see the error in my ways. In the spring of 2012, I was called in to help collaborate on a video project for an elementary school. This isn't unusual, as there is usually a campus or two that wants to work on something for their local community. However, this project was different, and I could tell from the beginning that it was going to be something that all kids, not just those at Eanes, could benefit from. The principal had sent me a song that I thought was commercially produced by some sort of Disney songwriter and singer. She explained to me that a couple of students had actually written a song as part of an anti-bullying project, and they recorded the song over the weekend (with the help of their uncle, a guitarist for pop singer Kelly Clarkson).

I met with a team of staff and the kids' parents in mid-April to discuss the possibility of making this into a music video. We listened to the song several times together as a group to get various ideas of how we wanted the video to look. My first thought when hearing the song, titled "Lend a Hand," was that kids would slowly start to join their cause throughout the video. The premise behind the song is that bystanders can be just as guilty as bullies and instead of standing idly by, they should lend a hand.

We had fifth graders develop vignettes for the verses of the song, and we plot pointed parts of the playground and areas around the campus to video record each vignette. Originally, the thought was that we would lip-sync the entire vocal part of the song in a single take. Although this can be tricky, it does make editing very easy (for me). I had some experience with this from other projects. However, in those video projects I shot that entire scene moving forward. This one would be the opposite, and require me to walk backwards, film, and give direction.

Needless to say, the ending footage wasn't very good. Here's a quick look at what that first draft looked like: http://tinyurl.com/q773ujd. Apologies if you get motion sick. As you will see, it is blurry, not in HD, and bouncy since I had to walk backwards.

I suddenly realized something. I was making this project a failure. Everyone involved up until that point had let the kids lead the experience and have their voice and choice in how it was delivered. The kids made the costumes. The kids designed the shirts. The kids planned and rehearsed the vignettes. The teachers and counselors let the kids have this freedom along the way to effectively promote their message of lending a hand. One factor was keeping this project from really getting off the ground, and I looked at him everyday in the mirror.

In the end, I decided to enlist the help of the Westlake broadcast journalism department and a couple of their aspiring videographers. While the idea of filming the whole song in sequence was still in my mind, they convinced me that we could shoot and edit it from two different angles with two different cameras, giving it more of a music video feel. These students also told me they could have it all edited and delivered to me in 48 hours and that I should "trust them" with the final results.

Being a person who has succeeded in life can be a hindrance. My own ego gets in the way of decisions all the time, and having these two teenagers ask me to trust them was a hard pill to swallow. Would they "see" my vision for this project? What if it turned out worse than my footage? In the end, I did trust them, and the final results left me humbled and also educated with a new concept—my ideas aren't always the best, and they can be improved on if I let others help. Or in this case, let others "lend a hand."

Here's the final music video project, which has since turned into a motto for the entire school: http://tinyurl.com/oweffv6. My children now attend the school and often come home wearing "Lend a Hand" t-shirts (see Figure 7.1) along with "Lend a Hand" stickers on their folders. All of this wouldn't have been possible if I didn't embrace a culture of shared ownership, risk taking and trust to let the students have a choice and a voice in their final learning outcomes.

This was a powerful moment in my own professional life, but also a powerful message to take to heart by anyone embarking on an initiative like this.

Figure 7.1 My oldest daughter modeling her "lend a hand" shirt.

CHAPTER 8

MODELING AND TRUST

At this point you've spent countless hours cultivating a culture of change and risk taking. You've brought in all the important stakeholders and leaders to buy into your mobile learning initiative. All of these actions are necessary to build community around mobile learning; however, don't underestimate the importance of your own actions as a leader.

Actions Speak Louder Than Words

Are you modeling all that you hope to accomplish in the classroom? If your district just became a Google Apps For Education (GAFE) district, are you using Google docs and regularly collaborating with others online? Or, are you still sending out Word doc attachments in all your emails and dumping materials and agenda minutes in a shared internal drive? While both may accomplish what you are looking for personally, what do these actions really show the other leaders and staff in your district?

It tells them that you want *them* to embrace this new collaborative world, but you will not actually be joining them on this journey. When we first began our iPad initiative, some school board members took it to heart and started showing up at every meeting with their own personal iPad in hand. In time, each board member was using an iPad as they sorted through slides and meeting notes. This may seem like a simple gesture, but it showed the community and staff that they not only support our mobile learning initiative, they actually believe in it enough to model it themselves.

As noted in the chapter about risk taking and failure, leaders are some of the most resistant to change. They are generally some of the most tenured people on a staff and have become very comfortable in the day-to-day roles they fulfill. Many superintendents and principals don't even attend the same professional learning they require their staff to attend! What does that say to those staff members? It says, "We think you should go and learn and continue to grow; however, we won't be alongside you for that."

One of the best workshops I ever had the pleasure of facilitating involved a staff of 120 teachers in McAllen ISD in south Texas. What made it so great? The room was filled with 80 teachers and support staff but also principals, assistant principals, and even the superintendent. When I've led or been a part of workshops in the past, the superintendent or principal will sometimes pop into the room for 5 or 10 minutes and maybe even say a few words. In the case of McAllen ISD, Dr. James Ponce didn't just attend—he was an active participant for the entire day.

Did he have other duties, meetings, or emails to get to? Sure. But his being a part of this day of learning with his staff and actively participating in it sent a loud message: Not only do I value this day for your learning, I value it enough to be here and learn alongside you.

When you are knee-deep in the planning and deployment stages of your mobile learning initiative, take a moment and personally reflect on your own actions. Although it won't be the thing that makes or breaks your initiative, modeling and being an active part of this change will help you earn the respect of your employees. Staff members are more apt to listen and follow a leader who is truly invested in the mission.

Substitute for a Day

One of my favorite activities as an administrator is actually teaching a class for a lesson or for a day. Most administrators in education spent some time in the classroom as a teacher. However, those days of Madeline Hunter lesson plan design and teacher-led daily lectures are long gone. I'm a fairly young administrator, but even I have been out of the classroom for more years now than I was in it.

I began teaching during the turn of the 21st century, but "21st-century learning" wasn't really a pressing item in our everyday teaching. My teaching strategy, even for a room full of 6-year-olds, was very much the same concept that we are stressing in the modern, mobile classroom. Students get a chance to have choice and voice in what they are learning. It's not about following directions as much as it is demonstrating your learning. We may not have had the mobile tools in my 2003 classroom, but we did have the only cart of Apple iBooks (the all-white models, not the tangerine-flavored ones) in the school. I saw firsthand how powerful truly higher-level integration of technology could be. My students were much more engaged in a project they had a vested interest in. When they had to design their own learning objectives based on their "passion project," it gave them a deeper understanding of their topics that I could never have gotten across in a traditional stand-and-deliver type lesson.

I'm recounting all of this not just for my own edification, but also to tell you, the reader, that all the cutting-edge and advanced learning theory I may have had in my first grade class 12 years ago has pretty much been flipped on it's head in a classroom with 1:1 mobile learning. Leaders of these initiatives make major decisions, gather input, and even share their successes, but how many of them have recently set foot in a classroom for longer than 10 minutes?

A better question would be, how many of them have actually taught in this modern classroom they have constructed? While administrators all have their fair share of "administrivia" to deal with on a daily basis, you should make time to visit a classroom at least once a week. Better yet, make time to come in and actually teach a lesson with the tools you have put in place. Modeling the use of technology is important, but I would say one of the most powerful forms of modeling it's use is actually teaching a lesson in a classroom full of kids. This can be both a humbling and rewarding experience, and it gives your words extra weight when you consider certain actions. Teachers (and parents) can smell a fraud. There's nothing quite like getting "messy in the learning" with your staff and students. It increases that level of respect and tells staff, "I wouldn't tell you to do something that I myself wouldn't do."

#Student4aday Challenge

Take the concept of subbing for a day a step further by actually being a student for a day. If administrators are years removed from the modern classroom experience, it's likely been decades since they have taken on the role of student in a school.

As an administrator, I'm faced with making decisions about major items on a daily basis. I spend time in meetings discussing and planning those decisions. I spend time speaking to parents about the rationale behind those decisions. And I train staff on the impact those decisions will have in their classrooms. However, the one group I felt I didn't have a strong enough grasp on was the most important group of all—the students. Becoming a student for a day meant that I got a small glimpse into what their daily academic life looked like. How did they use technology? How well did they interact in class with the teacher and with each other? How prevalent (and frequent) was their use of social media throughout the day? How uncomfortable were those desks they have to sit in?

It's because of these questions, and being inspired by my own education technologist Kacy Mitchell's challenge to be a middle school student for a day, that I decided in the fall of 2014 to place myself right in the middle of Westlake High School for a day. Before I embarked on the challenge, I made a few predictions and shared them on my blog. Following are some of those predictions.

1. **Kids will always be on their phones between classes.** I hear that this is always the case, so I wonder what it is they are doing. Is it just texting or are there selfies taking place all over? Will I be late to class if I participate?

2. **The desks will hurt my back.** I have an ergonomically correct chair in my office for lower lumbar support and a standing table for when I need to stand and type. That won't be an option during this challenge.

3. **Technology use will be a mixed bag.** While this schedule lends itself to some high-end technology use (I'll be in a couple of computer labs), I'm curious to see how much the iPad plays a role throughout the day—although the English teacher already emailed me to tell me it's a completely paperless assignment in his class, which makes my heart warm.

4. **My "real job" will affect my job as a student.** This might be the one prediction that will definitely come true. I'll have access to my email and I'll now be the "tech guy" in the classroom who can fix any technical problem. Hopefully, I'll be treated like a regular student, but just as in reality TV, that's not a real possibility.

Outcomes of #Student4aday

While I blogged and tweeted about my day as a student, reflecting on the entire experience really felt motivating and moving. I've been blessed to experience amazing professional development from around the world. I've had incredible, powerful conversations with people in my PLN via social media that help me learn and grow. All that said, my time as a student for a day was the most eye-opening and possibly most life-altering experience for me as an administrator in a public school.

Following are the outcomes of my predictions.

5. **Kids will be on their phones between classes.** Somewhat true. There were a few kids texting or listening to music or even talking on their phones (rarely), but for the most part, kids were talking to each other face to face. They were having conversations about a certain class, a movie, a game, or what they were doing after school. I assume some talked about relationships, too, but they tended to quiet down when I got close.

6. **The desks will hurt my back.** True. I suffer from mild back issues, but sitting in these torture contraptions was getting to be downright painful by the end of the day. I found myself fidgeting in them, turning to the side, slouching over, and generally just constantly shifting from one "cheek" to the other.

7. **Technology use will be a mixed bag.** True. In the English class it was extremely hands on, with the teacher using Nearpod to engage student questions about *Catcher in the Rye* and even having us draw what we thought Holden Caulfield looked like. Of course, the two computer lab courses heavily used technology as well. Most classes used the projector at a minimum; however, one class, Geometry, had a long-term sub, and so he was relegated to only using the dry-erase board. No technology (except for calculators) was allowed in that class.

8. **My "real job" will affect my job as a student.** I did miss fifth period for a meeting, and during U.S. History, I was asked to help troubleshoot with a Nearpod issue. I tried to claim I was just a regular high school kid, but the class cleverly remarked that most kids could help troubleshoot technology, so I should, too. Well played.

I share some of the components of this challenge in the hope that more administrators will participate in this ultimate level of higher-order modeling. Somewhere along the way in education we forget the reasons we do what we do. We do things for the students. We are swept up in meetings and conflicts and more meetings, and then something called a "deconflicting" meeting pops up and our lives are sent into a tailspin. We make decisions based on theory, but never actually live them or act them out. This challenge to be a student for a day is the ultimate eye-opening moment for witnessing the extensions of your actions and decisions as a leader.

Let the Group Decide

I mentioned a tactic in Chapter 2 that my superintendent uses when it comes to making a decision. He enlists the help of other stakeholders and gathers them around to discuss and troubleshoot a project. Then, when the time comes to make a final decision, he leaves the room and lets the group discuss it and deliver the message to him.

This not only empowers those in the room, but it also builds a level of trust between those in the room and himself. I tried this tactic recently around the decision behind a new learning management system (LMS). Our task force had met early to discuss nonnegotiables and goals for what our next LMS should have in terms of what we wanted to accomplish in our classrooms. Using these goals as our driving force, we piloted several models and then gathered feedback from students and teachers before heading into the final demo day.

On the day of the demos, I told the group of 15 or so staff who had been on this journey since the beginning that I would not be making the decision on that day. This left some of them perplexed. "Why did we spend all this time on this, then?" one of them asked. I told them that I wasn't finished. What I told them is that I wouldn't be the one making the decision—they would be.

In fact, I told them that to truly not have any influence on their decision, I would leave the room while they were deciding. I would give them all the back-end data, the surveys, the feedback, the rankings, but they would then make the ultimate decision, and I would support it no matter what.

When I left the room, I had a high level of anxiety because I suddenly had no control over what was being decided.

But then it hit me. I knew which platform I liked best as an administrator, but did that really matter? In the case of an LMS, the person using it the most is the student, followed closely by the teacher. So shouldn't the teacher and student have some say in that decision? I spent the rest of my time in isolation working on other projects until the group finally brought its decision to me. Although it may not have been what I would have done, it was much more thoughtful and grounded in reality for execution in the classroom. And in the end, that's much more important than my choosing what I like best.

CHAPTER 9

TYING IT ALL TOGETHER

We've looked at ways to cultivate change and risk taking. As a leader, you have modeled this new change in mobile learning and created a brand around your initiative. Getting buy-in and including stakeholders in the decision-making process gives everyone a sense of shared ownership. Now the tricky part—getting all the major players in this game to not only be on the same page, but also actually play nice with each other.

This chapter is dedicated to five main areas (and the subsequent books in this collection) that are necessary for making this initiative work: campus leadership; professional development; teaching and the learning environment; parents and community; and the technology services department. These are major cogs in the machine of mobile learning, and unless all of these components are working toward the same goal, the machine will struggle and eventually fail. Relying on all parts equally is ideal for running an initiative efficiently and with good mileage; however, there will be times when people in some areas will have to pull more than their own weight.

Campus Leadership

Dr. Anthony Muhammad has said that the person most likely to effect change and create a successful culture is the campus leader. A district leader can touch off amazing ideas and districtwide goals. However, without the support and ownership of the principal, those objectives can fall flat or even die before they get off the ground.

If you have a principal who is leading and pushing the campus to grow and improve, that attitude will go a long way to creating a successful culture built around mobile devices. Having a campus leader who is willing to be out in front and who truly believes in the initiative means that you'll have someone who is willing to take and handle pushback. This person will also push their staff to achieve greater heights in the name of the initiative.

Your role as a district leader is to identify those campus leaders with the most flexible and adaptable minds, while setting high expectations for staff to continue to grow and learn. Those leaders and campuses should be the first ones out in front during the pilot stages of your initiative. Not only will they set the bar high for other campuses to follow, they will also support and even push to make the initiative successful on their campus. Giving these leaders room to innovate and clearing roadblocks for them will go far beyond what you may have had in mind.

Professional Development

Having guidance and vision are key to communicating the goals and objective or the "why" of your mobile device initiative. Figuring out "the how" is of equal importance. Placing technology in the hands of teachers and students without training and support is a scenario fraught with failure.

A district leader should not see professional learning as optional in any scenario, much less one as costly as a mobile device initiative. I see it all the time. A district purchases X amount of hardware and then budgets for about 1/10th or less of that amount of money for support positions or training. Most successful private businesses allocate at least a third of their resources toward research, development, and training of staff. School districts can rarely afford to provide a high enough level of support to really transform the learning.

In my district, we scaled back our ed-tech positions because of state budget cuts right around the same time we were starting our pilot. To make the pilot a success, we made sure that a lot of time was allocated toward that single campus to really move the needle in terms of both support and integration. That also meant the rest of the district was temporarily neglected so we could focus our energy on getting this new initiative off to a good start. Because of that success, the pilot began to expand, and as a result of seeing the importance of having a strong team of professional educators helping with integration, we were able to hire back an educational technology expert for all nine buildings. Having the expert on hand means that learning can happen "just in time," and we can pool our talents to focus attention on one specific learning objective or campus.

Teaching and the Learning Environment

Much like campus leadership, how expectations are communicated are a huge part in making this a success. Communication should be a two-way street. Just handing down mandates and objectives from on high is a great way to sabotage the initiative before it even enters the classroom. I wrote at length in Chapter 7 about "shared ownership." This idea is especially valuable for teachers.

They are the ones having the most direct contact with our customers (students). What they say, what they allow to happen, and what they encourage will affect the learning outcomes in the classroom. A teacher who isn't on board or ready to change will resist until they no longer can. Others may jump at the chance to innovate and change for their students. The large majority of teachers in the middle could go either way. While it's natural to focus on those dragging their heels, I recommend that you focus on those teachers in the middle.

A big reason why we were able to expand our mobile learning initiative at the elementary level was because of the impassioned speech one of our more experienced teachers gave at a board meeting. She had just finished her 37th year of teaching and was not eager to try anything new, especially with technology. Reluctantly, she had the students try a writing project on their iPads, and the results as well as learning outcomes left her floored. Students were able to share and collaborate as she had never seen before. Her traditional way of doing the lesson may have achieved what she wanted, but the kids weren't learning a lot along the way. This discovery reinvigorated her own teaching style, and she was motivated to grow and learn because of it.

We needed to share her story and the stories of other teachers experiencing similar successes or struggles. As I mentioned in the chapter on modeling, a district leader should also experience these things firsthand and either attend or teach a lesson in a classroom. This has much more impact than discussing a theory or an idea about teaching and how the practice of education must change. Teaching experience gives you, as a leader, some shared respect.

Parents and Community

Our focus in education has always been (or at least, should always be) on the kids. They are the reasons the school building exists. However, we've blurred the lines in modern education between school and home. Once you start inviting technology into your school (via BYOD) or you start supplying the technology (via 1:1), you instantly put some pressure on parents not only to comply but also to be on board. I can't say it enough, but involving the community is probably one of the most, if not *the* most, vital factors in making a mobile device initiative a success.

Where most districts fail (and where we failed initially) is that thinking a "parent night" type meeting or newsletter would be enough to notify parents of this disruptive change. I use the word "disruptive" here not as hyperbole, but to drive home the point that many parents are not ready for the digital world that lies ahead for their teens. Whether you are leading a mobile device initiative or not, conversations about the digital world must be taking place from elementary through high school.

I feel that we as a district have improved from the unidirectional communication methods to more of a collaborative conversation with our parents around technology use and their kids. We also used this multi-channel communication as a teachable moment for our community. Many of today's adults were not raised in a world surrounded by digital devices. They are used to locking their doors at night, but not necessarily restricting their internet. They are accustomed to setting a curfew when kids need to be back home, yet they let their kids take devices into their bedroom and surf endlessly through all hours of the night.

While all this new technology represents disruption, many of the same parenting principles from the 20th century still apply. One of my proudest accomplishments was the creation of a Digital Parenting 101 iTunes U course (see Figure 9.1). I offered this course for three semesters in a row, and it has received some positive feedback and even elicited further face-to-face conversations and workshops.

The 2015 course had more than 130 parents in it from all over the world (I opened it up to the public after restricting the first two courses to Eanes parents). As an administrator, it's such a blessing to gain insight into the community's struggles with screen time, gaming addiction, and social media troubles. It helped me stay informed, and it prompted me to find resources to help parents in this digital era.

Figure 9.1 Digital Parenting 101

Technology Department

None of this works without the backing and support of your district technology department. It's next to impossible to have a successful mobile device initiative without the proper infrastructure or management of the devices. As a leader, you need to support this department, but you also need to make it clear that instruction and learning needs should be driving the decisions they make.

Too often I'll see a technology department create roadblocks to learning. Teachers will get excited about an idea to improve student engagement and learning, and the campus principal will support it, only to have it thrown back in their face as the technology department refuses to support anything new.

There is a belief in many technology departments that we are running "enterprise" systems in schools. While this may be true in concept, it fails in execution. Enterprise systems are useful in the business world, where every device is the same and all the software is identical. In schools that use technology effectively, the devices and software (i.e., tools) will vary based on the learning objective. You might have 27 students who need a particular app for learning about ecosystems, and you might have an entire course in need of software for their 3D printer. None of this is really enterprise or standard. Considering the fact that one of the driving forces behind mobile learning is differentiation and personalization, you can see how that could become a challenge to support.

Having spent two years in a technology department, I do sympathize with all this disruptive change. Most of the phone calls I received back then were about problems or issues with a particular piece of hardware or software. No one ever called just to say "Hey, just wanted to let you know that the network is running great!" or "My printer is working—just wanted to let you know." In a 1:1 environment, you drastically increase the number of customers and devices that you have to support. Add in the extra dynamic of parent support and complaints, and you can see how quickly a technology department can be taxed and overspent on helping support the initiative.

As I've said about teaching, it all comes back to the kids and learning. Someone not willing to change because it makes their own life harder is human and understandable. That does not make it excusable. The challenges that arise in a mobile learning initiative can be frustrating for all parties involved, but if the focus continues to be on student learning, those challenges change from problems to opportunities.

CHAPTER 10

REFLECTING AND SHARING

O nce you've made it through the first few stages of implementation, you will find yourself catching your breath and looking back at all you have accomplished. Although this isn't the end, you are finally on the road to true mobile learning in an effective way. The truth is, there is never an end to this journey—just various checkpoints and stops along the way.

Evaluate Where You Are

Overcoming challenges, bringing about change, and cultivating a shared ownership are not easy task. They require work and dedication to fully accomplish. The reality is, most staff are at different stages on your mobile learning journey. Although there will be moments when you see a light at the end of the proverbial tunnel, the truth is that there are more tunnels ahead.

So although you should truly reflect on and enjoy the monumental change you have brought to your schools, you also need to evaluate where you are on the journey as a whole, and what the next steps should be. As mentioned in the previous chapter, there are many components to this machine of mobile learning, and each one is at a different stage of readiness or excellence. You might have parents completely on board with the concept, but teachers are reluctant to change. Perhaps your technology department is open and adaptable to different ideas, but you don't have funding or time for proper professional development.

Whatever the case may be, it's valuable to have some form of reflection or feedback that the staff, students, and community can participate in. A simple survey can be a powerful set of data points, but if you really want to stretch your goals (remember that chapter on taking risks!), why not try something a little different?

The "Un-Committee"

The beauty of writing this book now is that we are actually currently heading into the next phase of our mobile device initiative. In the summer of 2016 (one year from this writing), our district will be rolling out our second phase of 1:1. Our current devices have lasted four or five years, and a lot has changed since the initial pilot.

Some immediate questions that have come up as a result of this refresh are: How have we done thus far? What device should be next? Should they all be the same? Certainly, these are questions in need of answers, and some surveys could gather that feedback. However, that's too easy. Our board has asked that we form a "Technology Advisory Committee." Believe what you might about committees, but in reality they are a great way to give a minority a powerful voice while displacing blame down the road.

In this age of technology and innovative thinking, why do schools (and companies) still revert to the voices of a few "randomly" chosen people to make decisions? It seems that it would make more sense to crowdsource information from multiple inputs and then deaggregate all that data to make a more informed decision.

Another major problem with committees is that all too often they are composed of people with an axe to grind, people looking for power, or people who are uninformed by the countless hours of research and development that staff members have spent on the topic. They will come into the committee with their own preconceived notions and an "angle" based on some limited knowledge.

Knowing that totally scrapping a committee would be a tough sell, I decided to formulate a plan. Why not take this as an opportunity to not only inform and educate the community but also get loads of data points to make a more authentic and well-thought-out decision? So, in the fall of 2015 we embarked on a series of "Digital Learning Symposiums."

These symposiums are accompanied by a "task force" (much more powerful and temporary than a committee) whose members attend each sympo- sium and gather data to present to the district for our next round of mobile learning. The symposiums include site visits to 1:1 classrooms in action, student and teacher panels, and visits by experts to reveal what the future may hold for our students. Within each symposium (which is open to the public and recorded for online viewing later), there is a chance for audience interac- tion and communication. Some of this is done digitally via a backchannel, while other parts are handled the "old-fashioned" way with paper and sticky notes (and then captured digitally).

While some administrators or leaders may dread these sorts of events, I look forward to them. They give me the opportunity to reflect not only on how far we have come, but also on how much further we still have to go. They also provide some "covert" education for our community, as they will learn a lot more about our mobile learning initiative from seeing it in action and hearing the research behind it.

Reevaluate Expectations

Speaking of reflecting and seeing how much further we have to go, expectations around a mobile learning initiative need to be constantly evolving. We are a district that has high achievement scores, and 99% of our students are accepted into a two- or four-year college. Westlake High School was recently ranked as the number one high school in the state of Texas and in the top 20 in the country (https://k12.niche.com/westlake-high-school-austin-tx) So, with all of this success, why would we ever change?

In 2013, we had the pleasure of having Dr. Anthony Muhammad (http://newfrontier21.com/consulting/anthony) speak to our entire staff during a convocation event. Dr. Muhammad speaks mainly on the topic of school culture, and one of the things he said during his keynote speech that really stuck with me was his statement that there is no ceiling on excellence.

When I mentioned earlier that there truly is no end for this journey, his quote primarily guides that statement. No matter how far you go with mobile learning, there will always be more to accomplish and more to achieve, because the world is always evolving. Powerful, authentic learning in this new generation of devices is a moving target. You'll want to set mini-goals along the way to gauge success, but know that the end goal will always be just beyond your reach—if you are doing this right.

Share What You Have Learned

If a tree falls in the forest and no one is around to hear it, did it make a noise? This old saying has been around for generations, but I think we can apply a similar one to being a leader during a mobile learning initiative. If you learn something but don't share it, did it really happen? As Patrick Larkin mentioned during his interview in Chapter 3, we are doing a disservice to others in education if we don't share our successes, and probably even more importantly, our failures.

Much like mobile devices, social media is a part of our everyday lives. We have a bevy of ways to communicate but also connect. When I started research on our 1:1 initiative in 2010, Twitter was just coming into prominence. I was lucky enough to get started early on Twitter, making connections and learning from those who had paved the road before me. A few weeks before we began our pilot, I was on a Skype call with an administrator of a 1:1 school in Brazil, and moments later I was chatting on Twitter with a leader in the state of Maine, whose statewide mobile learning initiative really paved the way for other districts and states in the early 2000s (http://maine.gov/mlti). Documenting what you learn along this journey helps with reflection, but blogging about it also shows that you are "learning out loud" in a sense. Others are able to patch into your reflections and use them to help with their own initiatives. This book series was in fact born out of this desire to share best practices, real-world examples, and failures to avoid.

So, for those of you moving forward down the path of mobile learning, I beg you to not only document all you do, but share it with others who are following you. You never know what impact you might have on student learning, even for students in schools that are not your own.

Predicting the Future

Vision can mean multiple things, but the best definition in the case of this book is "the act or power of anticipating that which will or may come to be" (http://dictionary.reference.com/browse/vision). Your job as a visionary leader is to in fact predict the future and act on it. As we discussed in the chapter on risk taking, that could mean some epic failure. However, I'd argue that not taking a risk and moving to change could also be an epic failure.

The truth of the matter is that we can't see the future, especially in the world of technology. In the four years since our initiative started, we have seen things such as drones, wearables, 3D printers, and the "internet of things" (http://en.wikipedia.org/wiki/Internet_of_Things) arise in our world and in education. One thing we can predict with 100% accuracy is that the future will be different. I will also say with 99% confidence that technology will play a key part in what shapes the future world.

Knowing this means that whatever innovations we decide to make, we need to make sure they are adaptable and flexible. They need to be effective and efficient, but they also need to help with students' learning at a holistic level. The change needs to improve their learning, their future, their chances for success, and most importantly, their lives.

We might not know what tools will be needed to make that happen, but we need to have the vision to know that whatever those tools may be, we will dedicate our time and our craft to making this happen for our "customers," the students.

ISTE STANDARDS

The ISTE Standards for Administrators (ISTE Standards·A)

All school administrators should be prepared to meet the following standards and performance indicators.

1. **Visionary Leadership**

   Administrators inspire and lead development and implementation of a shared vision for comprehensive integration of technology to promote excellence and support transformation throughout the organization. Administrators:

   a. Inspire and facilitate among all stakeholders a shared vision of purposeful change that maximizes use of digital age resources to meet and exceed learning goals, support effective instructional practice and maximize performance of district and school leaders.

   b. Engage in an ongoing process to develop, implement and communicate technology-infused strategic plans aligned with a shared vision.

   c. Advocate on local, state and national levels for policies, programs and funding to support implementation of a technology-infused vision and strategic plan.

2. Digital Age Learning Culture

Administrators create, promote and sustain a dynamic, digital age learning culture that provides a rigorous, relevant and engaging education for all students. Administrators:

a. Ensure instructional innovation focused on continuous improvement of digital age learning.

b. Model and promote the frequent and effective use of technology for learning.

c. Provide learner-centered environments equipped with technology and learning resources to meet the individual, diverse needs of all learners.

d. Ensure effective practice in the study of technology and its infusion across the curriculum.

e. Promote and participate in local, national and global learning communities that stimulate innovation, creativity and digital age collaboration.

3. Excellence in Professional Practice

Administrators promote an environment of professional learning and innovation that empowers educators to enhance student learning through the infusion of contemporary technologies and digital resources. Administrators:

a. Allocate time, resources and access to ensure ongoing professional growth in technology fluency and integration.

b. Facilitate and participate in learning communities that stimulate, nurture and support administrators, faculty and staff in the study and use of technology.

c. Promote and model effective communication and collaboration among stakeholders using digital age tools.

    d. Stay abreast of educational research and emerging trends regarding effective use of technology and encourage evaluation of new technologies for their potential to improve student learning.

4. Systemic Improvement

Administrators provide digital age leadership and management to continuously improve the organization through the effective use of information and technology resources. Administrators:

    a. Lead purposeful change to maximize the achievement of learning goals through the appropriate use of technology and media-rich resources.

    b. Collaborate to establish metrics, collect and analyze data, interpret results and share findings to improve staff performance and student learning.

    c. Recruit and retain highly competent personnel who use technology creatively and proficiently to advance academic and operational goals.

    d. Establish and leverage strategic partnerships to support systemic improvement.

    e. Establish and maintain a robust infrastructure for technology including integrated, interoperable technology systems to support management, operations, teaching and learning.

5. Digital Citizenship

Administrators model and facilitate understanding of social, ethical and legal issues and responsibilities related to an evolving digital culture. Administrators:

    a. Ensure equitable access to appropriate digital tools and resources to meet the needs of all learners.

    b. Promote, model and establish policies for safe, legal and ethical use of digital information and technology.

c. Promote and model responsible social interactions related to the use of technology and information.

d. Model and facilitate the development of a shared cultural understanding and involvement in global issues through the use of contemporary communication and collaboration tools.

© 2012 International Society for Technology in Education (ISTE), iste.org. All rights reserved.

REFERENCES

Estrin, J. (2008). *Closing the innovation gap: Reigniting the spark of creativity in the global economy.* New York: McGraw-Hill.

Fullan, M. (2001) *Leading in a culture of change.* Retrieved from www.csus.edu/indiv/j/jelinekd/edte%20227/fullanleadinginacultureofchange.pdf

Laura Wright's Third Grade Class (2013). *The Life of an Eanes Pioneer Child* [iTunes version]. Retrieved from https://itunes.apple.com/us/book/life-eanes-pioneer-child/id595702755?mt=11

Niche (2015). *Best K–12 schools: 2015 Niche rankings.* Retrieved from https://k12.niche.com/westlake-high-school-austin-tx

Puentadura, R. (n.d.). *SAMR: Methods for transforming the classroom.* Retrieved from www.hippasus.com/rrpweblog/archives/2013/10/25/SAMR_MethodsForTransformingTheClassroom.pdf

Sinek, S. (2009). *TED Talk: How great leaders inspire action.* Retrieved from www.ted.com/talks/simon_sinek_how_great_leaders_inspire_action

Wujec, T. (2010). *TED Talk: Build a tower, build a team.* Retrieved from http://marshmallowchallenge.com/Welcome.html